The Joan Baez Songbook

THE JOAN BAEZ SONGBOOK

ARRANGEMENTS AND INTRODUCTION BY

ELIE SIEGMEISTER

PREFACE BY JOHN M. CONLY

ILLUSTRATED BY ERIC VON SCHMIDT

EDITED BY MAYNARD SOLOMON

MUSIC EDITORS:

CHRISTA LANDON & JACK LOTHROP

AMSCO PUBLICATIONS
NEW YORK/LONDON/SYDNEY

Acknowledgments

We have made every effort to determine the copyright status of the songs included herein. We wish to thank the publishers of the following songs for permission to reprint their copyrighted material. This book could not have been prepared without their kind cooperation.

"The Tramp On The Street." Words and music by Grady and Hazel Cole. Copyright 1940 and 1947 by Dixie Music Pub. Co.

"We Shall Overcome." New Words and music arrangement by Zilphia Horton, Frank Hamilton, Guy Carawan and Pete Seeger. Copyright 1960 and 1963 by Ludlow Music, Inc., New York, NY. Used by permission. Royalties derived from this composition are being contributed to the Freedom Movement under the trusteeship of the writers.

"Last Night I Had The Strangest Dream." Words and music by Ed McCurdy. Copyright 1950 and 1955 by Almanac Music, Inc., New York, NY. Used by permission.

"The Ranger's Command." Words and music by Woody Guthrie. Copyright 1963 by Ludlow Music, Inc., New York, NY. Used by permission.

"Copper Kettle" (or, "The Pale Moonlight"). Words and music Albert F. Beddoe. Copyright 1960 and 1963 by Melody Trails, Inc., New York, NY Used by permission.

"Black Is The Color." By John Jacob Niles. Copyright 1936 and 1963 by G. Schirmer, Inc. New York, NY. Reprinted by permission.

"I Never Will Marry." Words and music by Fred Hellerman. Copyright 1958 by Sanga Music, Inc. New York, NY.

"Danger Waters." Copyright Arthur S. Alberts, 1949, Field Recordings, 1950. Riverside Records 1953; Words and Music by Jacob Brown. All Rights Reserved. Used by permission.

"Where Have All The Flowers Gone." Words and music by Peter Seeger. Inspired by a passage from Mikhail Sholokhov's novel,

"And Quiet Flows The Don." Copyright 1961 by Fall River Music, Inc., New York, NY.

"What Have They Done To The Rain." Words and music by Malvina Reynolds. Copyright 1962 by Schroder Music Co. Used by permission.

"Donna Donna" (or "Dona Dona"). Music by Sholom Secunda, words by Aaron Zeitlin. Copyright 1940 and 1963 by Mills Music, copyright owner. International copyright secured. Used by permission of the copyright owner. English lyrics used in this book by Arthur Kevess and Teddi Schwartz, copyright 1956 by Hargail Music Press. Used by permission.

"Portland Town." Words and music by Derroll Adams. Copyright 1957 by Sing Out! Inc. Copyright assigned 1964 to Ryerson Music Publishers, Inc. All rights reserved. Used by permission.

"Babe I'm Gonna Leave You." Words and music by Anne H. Braden—by assignment from Janet Smith. Copyright 1963 by Ryerson Music Publishers, Inc. Used by permission.

"Long Black Veil." By Marijon Wilkins and Danny Dill. Copyright 1959 by Cedarwood Publishing Co., Inc., 815 16th Avenue South, Nashville, TN. All rights reserved. International copyright secured.

"Ten Thousand Miles" (or, "Fare Thee Well"). Words and music by David Gude. Copyright 1960 by Sanga Music, Inc., New York, NY.

"Stewball." By Robert Yellin, John Herald and Ralph Rinzler. Copyright 1961 and 1963 by Ryerson Music Publishers, Inc., New York, NY.

"John Riley." By Bob Gibson and Ricky Neff. Copyright 1961 by Sanga Music, Inc. and Harvard Music, Inc., New York, NY. Used by permission.

"Pretty Boy Floyd." Words and music by Woody Guthrie. Copyright 1961 by Fall River Music, Inc., New York, NY.

Order No. AM 10455
International Standard Book Number: 0.8256.2611.0
Library of Congress Catalog Card Number: 64-24388

Exclusive Distributors:
Music Sales Corporation
257 Park Avenue South, New York, NY 10010, USA.
Music Sales Limited
14-15 Berners Street, London W1T 3LJ, UK.
Music Sales Pty Limited
20 Resolution Drive, Caringbah, NSW 2229, Australia.

Printed in Great Britain

TO MY MOTHER AND FATHER
WITH LOVE,
—JOANIE

Joan Baez by John M. Conly

The paramount fact about Joan Baez is beauty. She has it; she generates it; and she uses it. Lest this seem rhapsodical, be it admitted that she is a human being, with impulses, frailties, and foibles, perhaps even a little young wickedness. But the gospel is beauty.

So is the person, and not only vocally. Were it her wish, she could easily produce the same sort of visual impact as did, say, Audrey Hepburn at the same age. At close view, she seems contrived of a sort of dark sunlight. The skin was made to consort with bright colors; the dusk of the long hair is like a shadow in a canyon. The eyes are a deep topaze, very steady. The face is slender, strong, aquiline, and secret. There is a slight sardonic curl to her lips, even at rest; it is a lovely mouth but not peaceful. Even silently, it speaks of a world she may want to love, but has trouble liking.

Plainly she has no desire to appear a conventional beauty. Indeed, she dresses against any such possibility. Her admirers waggishly advert to her concert costumes as gunny sacks. They aren't, quite, but they are commonly handwoven garb, purposely shapeless, so that she seems almost a twig-legged waif, a grown-up Little Match Girl, in the spotlight. Offstage she is not in the least twiggy. She has a fine, lithe dancer's body. One has the impression that she would fence very well (as, metaphorically, against the everyday world, she does). She is vividly alert.

She is a personage, of which she is aware. Or, rather, perhaps, she may think of herself as a purpose, of which she has been given charge whether she wants it or not. She is conscious of her image. At an artist's studio, during the preparation of this book, she idly moved behind his drawing board and, half-doodling, sketched a picture (she draws very well and quickly). It was a Joan Baez. More to the point, it was a stylized Joan Baez, with tresses flowing forward over the shoulders, a young mystery. This is her image, and do not read the word in the Madison Avenue sense. It is not an image she created for any public; it is truly the image she has found, thus far, looking for Joan Baez. She offers it honestly.

She offers it, also, with love. Love and beauty are indivisible —in her singing, her living, her view of the world. There is consummate musicality in her art, but the word seems to trouble her, and she would rather call it loving.

Here we come to a dichotomy. Joan Baez is not two persons, but she has two aspects, both important. For one thing, here is a truly lucent voice, vital and lofting, with a timbre that is a resistless distillate of poignancy and pure thrill. She can sing "Copper Kettle," a boozy ditty of rustic laziness, in a way to make it search souls, almost incredibly. This is a natural gift, a built-in concord of brain and vocal cords, that will never leave her. It is plain musicality, and would work with or without loving.

Besides this, and not apart from it, is Joan Baez, 23, a young woman grown suddenly consequential to a whole sector of today's humanity, by reason of her beauty in another way, i.e., what she does with it.

Joan Baez has no wish to be a leader, an emblem, or a spokesman, and she is none. She is rather, an object, a focus of feelings; and, actively, one who tends with tenderness. She is part of a sort of elite corps of today's young. They have emerged from childhood into a world which seems to them disorganized to the point of dreadfulness, almost beyond grasp or hope. They are not beatniks nor even Angry Young Men; they are too thoughtful and humane for that. They are at once responsible and baffled. And, in very dubious battle, they need consolidation, they need emotional focus, and they sorely need comfort—the ultimate, unbreakable comfort that is found only in beauty and simplicity.

She says of them, not excluding herself: "They have to find out who they are, what they are, before they can do anything." Their tastes distinguish them (though this can be oversimplified). They read J. D. Salinger; the poetry of Allen Ginsberg; in some cases the suspirative science-fantasy of Ray Bradbury; and William Golding's The Lord of the Flies. Some of them have sat through David and Lisa twice. And they have gravitated en masse to folk music, and their favorite is Joan Baez.

This is natural; she is — for what she is — perfection, and they are perfectionists. There is not an ounce of compromise in them. They want a better world; that is that. An odd sidelight of this (to their elders, one of whom is writing this), is that it would seem to be, this ideal world, altogether young. One has the feeling that they so distrust today's elders, for what they have done, or not done, that they do not even want to think of themselves at fifty or sixty, or perhaps as being fifty or sixty. Perhaps it would not be a bad thing for the world, at that, if some of the feelings of twenty-two could last a whole lifetime.

At that, their demands aren't exorbitant, at least Joan's aren't. When asked (offhand and unfairly) what she would do to bring about the better world, she said simply: "End war, and let the people involved with it go to some useful work." And added wryly: "Including picketers and folksingers!"

It is probably wrong to call her a folksinger. She is a singer, mainly of folk songs, because she loves them. As she sings them, however, they are (what critics call) art-songs; there is little genre flavor. To her they are at their best when most beautiful, refined and intelligible. This is a principle shared with her, almost uniquely, by Richard Dyer-Bennet. The difference is that a Dyer-Bennet evening is historical; the listener is transported, with familiar ease, to other times and climes. With Joan Baez, history happens now. The identification is brought to the listener, he needn't go after it. The translation is complete. An ethnically-minded folklorist said once of her that she can make any song sound as if it were being sung by Joan Baez. What this acid wit missed was the point. Joan Baez remains Joan Baez. When character-identification in a song is not possible—as in the pirate chronicle, "Henry Martin"—she becomes Joan Baez, musical story-teller.

Joan Baez is of Mexican and Scottish-Irish parentage, and her father is a rather noted scientist and educator. She has lived in a number of places, mostly cities, and has been exposed to all the education she wanted. However, folk song was her own discovery, in her late teens (remember, she is precocious). Patently it filled a want in her. She has not said this, but her work shows it (as does this book): it offered her a sort of kinship with the continuing "condition humaine," the changeless part of man's nature; the sensitivity, humor, bravery, acceptance, and shrewdness that have sustained our kind in all ages and quarters of the world—and which we need now.

Joan Baez has purveyed this, beautifully, with her voice and her presence. Now she continues the effort with this book. It would seem highly likely that anyone who buys this book already owns at least one Joan Baez record. Anyone who doesn't: buy one. However, do not try to imitate her singing. In the first place, you can't. In the second place, that is not what she offers this book for. You are supposed to discover your own way into the songs, as she did. It should be a lovely adventure.

Table of Contents

Table of Contents

Folk Music: The Long View by Elie Siegmeister

A long time ago, when I first became interested in American folk music, my friends considered it an eccentricity. I had studied conducting at the Juilliard School for several years and had come to a trusted advisor with the idea that I would make my conducting debut leading a group of singers in an evening of American folk music at Town Hall.

"American folk music," my friend said with compassion, "Who would come to hear it?"

Nowadays one cannot set foot in a high school lunch room anywhere in these states without hearing the twanging guitar of the local Burl Ives, nor visit a cafe anywhere in Europe without being aware of an American cowboy song or a blues coming over the radio — in Swedish, Dutch, or Italian, of course.

What accounts for this astonishing growth of a new music in the short space of a single generation — or, more accurately, of the rebirth of a centuries-old music just when it was about to die out?

The answer is not simple, but among other things, in the 1930's and '40's, there were the New Deal and the anti-fascist war — movements that awakened the humane instincts of all of us. In a period when millions were deprived, disinherited, and then destroyed, there was a need for an affirmation of things basically human. It was a time when intellectual people felt drawn to a commonality with others whose lives and rights were threatened with extinction. I remember vividly the excitement of such expressions as Marc Blitzstein's Cradle Will Rock, Gershwin's Porgy and Bess, Steinbeck's Grapes of Wrath, the Federal Theater's Living Newspapers.

The discovery of folk music by a generation of young musicians and composers was more than another fad — it opened up a new meaning for American music as a whole. For now those of us who were just starting out could feel part of a rich tradition; we could feel like new branches on an old tree — and this strengthened us. The need for roots that every artist senses sooner or later was particularly strong at that time; many of us knew we could be more ourselves in an American language than in one fathered in Paris, Vienna, or Berlin.

When, therefore, I first met Aunt Molly Jackson, the time was ripe; I was enchanted by her at once. It was after one of those concerts organized by a few indigent musicans calling ourselves The Young Composers Group, at the New School, New York, early in 1933. The program notes proclaimed boldly that we were the start of a new American music (as all program notes of such groups do — and should do). After the concert, our relatives, who comprised the majority of the audience, came back to congratulate us; but among them was this strange, raggedy woman with a hawk-like face: she came right up to me and said "You think you are writing American music — did you ever hear any real American music?" After trading a few insults, we each became fascinated by the ideas of the other. Result: Aunt Molly asked me if I would care to write down some of the few hundred songs she had "composed," and I said I would.

I did.

I was but one of many composers who responded to the currents of the time. In the early '30s we all knew of the great work of Charles Ives, then something of a legendary figure, but nonetheless a mighty pioneer in the use of folk material. His "Charlie Rutlage," "General Booth Enters Heaven," his Violin and Piano Sonatas, his Concord Sonata for Piano loomed as brilliant and imaginative evocations of American life, with fragments of minstrel songs, ragtime, folk music, and jazz interwoven into their complex fabric. Henry Cowell and Charles Seeger were preaching the folk music gospel at the New School. John Lomax, Alan Lomax, Ben Botkin, and others were out in the field collecting hundreds of recordings for the Library of Congress. Virgil Thomson wrote one of the first movie scores using the folk idiom, The Plough That Broke the Plains. In addition to young men such as Jerome Moross, Alex North, and myself, members of the "arrived" generation of Douglas Moore and Aaron Copland were making rich use of the ballad and cowboy idiom in movie, theater, and ballet scores.

My greatest adventure with folk music came in the early forties when simultaneously I conducted concerts of the American Ballad Singers, wrote a score for the first folk musical to appear on Broadway, Sing Out Sweet Land, and composed Ozark Set.

Among the strongest folk musicians then beginning to be heard around in village cafes, anti-Nazi and pro-Spanish loyalist meetings were Josh White, Woody Guthrie, The Almanac Singers, Burl Ives, and of course, Leadbelly. After a certain amount of exposure, it was inevitable that a bit of audience appeal crept into the performances of some, but Leadbelly was solid as a rock. He neither could nor would be moved to do anything other than sing his repertory exactly as he always had sung it: deadpan, with a gravelly voice that was beautiful, and a guitar rhythm that shook the walls.

Gradually the folk music movement spread out. New performers came on the scene: Pete Seeger, Oscar Brand, Jean Ritchie, The Weavers, Tom Scott, and many others. Collections and books have come off the presses each year: after the pioneering works of Cecil Sharp and John Lomax, there appeared the Carl Sandburg book, those of Alan Lomax, Ben Botkin, Lawrence Gellert, John Jacob Niles, Olin Downes' and my own Treasury of American Song and dozens and dozens more.

The influence of folk music on American composers did not originate yesterday. There is more than a trace of folk rhythms and song patterns in many choruses of William Billings, a contemporary of Paul Revere and Samuel Adams. In the mid-1800's it was not only Stephen Foster, Daniel Emmett, Cool White, and other minstrel song-writers who revealed the influences of folk syncopation and melodic inflections; there was that picaresque character, Louis Gottschalk, whose piano pieces show that the tango, rhumba, and ragtime beats date back more than a hundred years.

But the most marked change came with Ives at the turn of the century and, more than thirty years later, with the New Deal generation of Gershwin, Thomson, Copland, Blitzstein, Moore, Gould, Moross, North, and myself among others. It was not an accident that American music — like French, German, Russian, Hungarian music before it—took on distinctive character and emerged on the world scene at the very moment that the life-blood of folk music entered the art of serious composers. American sonatas, symphonies, operas, theater and ballet scores sprang to life at the same time as folk music was winning wide recognition as a native art.

In recent years this trend took another turn. The Cold War created a new phenomenon: Cold Art. The feelings of enthusiasm and faith in an ideal that moved many artists in the years 1930-45 gradually fell away, and were replaced by a deep unbelief, a corrosion of feeling, a shying away of one human being from another. Two quite contradictory effects emerged: the loss of interest in folk music by serious musicians, and the enormous growth of interest in it by the people as a whole. In the post-World War II period there arose the deep need for a human affirmation in a time of anxiety. Without a clear ideal of life, the young people of our time have turned to the universal expression that is folk music.

The elemental themes represented by the songs in this collection, ranging from old Child Ballads, newer Anglo-American ballads, mountain love songs, country and western tunes, hymns and Spirituals and topical songs of today bring the singer and listener closer to the sources of American music: the spontaneous creation of many generations of the plain people of our country.

The eagerness of vast numbers of folk music enthusiasts to sing and play these songs is evidence of a reaction against the passivity induced by ready-made entertainment. The very roughness of folk performance speaks as a bulwark against the slickness of pre-fabricated commercial art. It affirms a desire to participate actively once more in the expression of a genuine and meaningful human experience. Perhaps it is a precursor of a similar swing of the pendulum among our serious musicians who have turned this way and that, and who may once again note the musical voice of our own time and people.

The chord progressions indicated above the music are the chords as they sound in the key in which the arrangement is written. Following these are chords in parentheses which are the chords actually played when a capo is used to avoid the more difficult bar chords.

For the guitarist who wishes to play along with the Joan Baez recordings, which are often in different keys than the keys of the piano arrangements, we have supplied a legend above each song, as for example:

  Key: E   Capo: 4th   Play: C

This means that Joan Baez sings this song in the key of E; that the capo is to be placed at the 4th fret; that the player is to finger the chords as if they were in C, but that they will actually sound in E.

Occasionally, the harmony of the piano arrangement differs from Joan Baez' guitar accompaniment. In these cases, Joan's harmony is indicated by a footnote, so that the pianist who wishes to observe her original chord progressions can do so.

The editors have refrained from suggesting any "picking" styles, preferring to leave that choice up to the guitarist.

For the Guitarist

About the Contributors

Elie Siegmeister, born in New York City in 1909, is a distinguished American composer who, throughout his career, has been interested in American folk music both in its original form and as source material for musical composition in larger forms. Among his achievements in this area are the Broadway musical, "Sing Out Sweet Land"; "Ozark Set", which was performed by major symphony orchestras and recorded by Dimitri Mitropoulos; and "Western Suite", which was premiered by Arturo Toscanini and the NBC Symphony in 1945. Siegmeister has also attained distinction in the fields of absolute music and vocal works on tragic themes. His long list of compositions includes three symphonies, two string quartets, violin and piano sonatas, "A Strange Funeral in Braddock" and a full-length opera based on Sean O'Casey's "The Plough and the Stars."

Eric von Schmidt has been active as a painter, graphic artist and illustrator for almost fifteen years. He was awarded a Fulbright to Italy in 1955-6, and has given seven one-man shows of his paintings. As a folksinger, he has become a major figure in the blues revival, and has recorded for Folkways Records and Prestige Folklore. It was as a folksinger that he first met Joan Baez when she was beginning her career in Cambridge in 1958-9, and the illustrations for this book are the result of their long friendship. Von Schmidt has two daughters, Caitlin and Megan, and has recently begun to write as well as illustrate books for young people. The first two, "Come for to Sing" and "The Young Man Who Wouldn't Hoe Corn", will soon be followed by "The Ballad of Bad Ben Bilge."

John Marsland Conly was born in Manhattan to a pair of newspaper people who had started as English teachers. At the age of eleven, he recalls, he was a fairly reliable authority on the fauna of the Mesozoic Era, meaning mainly dinosaurs. At fifteen he was a promising painter. He moved briefly into the field of scholarship and taught history at the University of Rochester for one year. He could not keep away from typewriters, however, a family failing. In 1940 he went to work for the New York Herald Tribune. Since then he has been in succession a police reporter, a science columnist, music editor of The Atlantic Monthly and editor of High Fidelity. Conly is now, at the age of fifty, a free lance writer. He contributes an intermittent column to The Reporter and is working on three books at once.

LYRICS
AND
LAMENTS

Folksongs generally can be classified into two groups; ballads (narrative folksongs) and lyrics (emotive non-narrative songs). The two species are not as distinctly separate as one might believe, however, for many lyric folksongs have derived wholly from ballads. When most of the narrative details are sheared away from ballads what remains is the emotional core, the essence to be found in many of the best lyric folksongs and laments. Other lyric pieces are simply a conglomeration of floating folk commonplace verses, lines and phrases, forming one combination here and another there. Their extreme beauty, in isolation or in combination, often compares favorably with the finest art poetry in any language.

The verses of this lyric dialogue from the Appalachians may once have been part of a ballad, but all that remains is a comment on frustrated love. Such lines are frequently found in combination with other equally beautiful ones (see for example those of "Rambler Gambler"), though they lose little in isolation as witnessed by the five short verses of this piece. Joan Baez sings it without accompaniment.

Wagoner's Lad

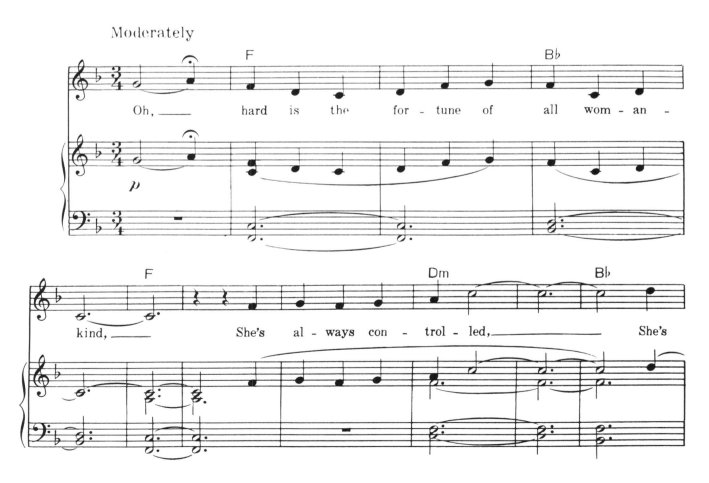

Moderately

Oh, _____ hard is the for - tune of all wom - an - kind, _____ She's al - ways con - trol - led, _____ She's

al - ways con - fined, ___ Con - trolled by her par - ents___ ___ un - til she's a wife, _____ A___ slave to her hus - band the rest of her life. _____

2. Oh, I'm just a poor girl,
        my fortune is sad,
   I've always been courted
        by the wagoner's lad,
   He's courted me daily,
        by night and by day,
   And now he is loading
        and going away.

3. Oh, my parents don't like him,
        because he is poor,
   They say he's not worthy
        of entering my door,
   He works for a living,
        his money's his own,
   And if they don't like it,
        they can leave him alone.

4. "Oh, your horses are hungry,
        go feed them some hay,
   Then sit down here by me,
        as long as you may."
   "My horses ain't hungry,
        they won't eat your hay,
   So fare thee well darlin',
        I'll be on my way."

5. "Oh, your wagon needs greasing,
        your whip is to mend,
   Then sit down here by me,
        as long as you can."
   "My wagon is greasy,
        my whip's in my hand,
   So fare thee well darlin',
        no longer to stand."

This sorrowful cry of a lonesome man has been found in various parts of the southern mountains. Its verses consist of a series of variations on a theme—a heart-rending one at that. Occasionally the first line reads "I am a maid . . ." or "I am a girl . . .," but even without the change in sex the song sings well by women.

Man of Constant Sorrow

KEY: C   CAPO: NONE   PLAY: C

Moderately slow

G (G, etc.)   C

I am a man ———— of con-stant sor-row, ———— And I've seen

Am   Dm

trou - - bles all my days.   I'll bid fare-

well _____ to old Ken - tuck - y, _____ The state where

first and others   *last time*

I _____ was born and raised. _____ 2. All through this raised. _____

2.   All through this world I'm bound to ramble,
      Through sun and wind and driving rain,
      I'm bound to ride the Northern Railway,
      Perhaps I'll take the very next train.

3.   Your friends may think that I'm a stranger,
      My face you'll never see no more,
      There is a promise that is given,
      I'll see you on God's golden shore.

4.   I always thought I had seen trouble
      Now I know it's common run
      I'll hang my head and weep in sorrow
      Just to think on what you've done.

5.   And when I'm in some lonesome hour,
      And I am feeling all alone,
      I'll weep the briny tears of sorrow
      And think of you so far a-gone.

6.   Oh, I'm a man of constant sorrow, etc.

Lady Mary

The text of this song has an Elizabethan ring to it, but it comes from the Ozark Mountains where Vance Randolph collected it from May Kennedy McCord. One would think that such an exquisite text and tune would be found more widely in tradition, but to date no other version of this lyric has turned up on either side of the Atlantic.

KEY: C#   CAPO: 4TH   PLAY: A

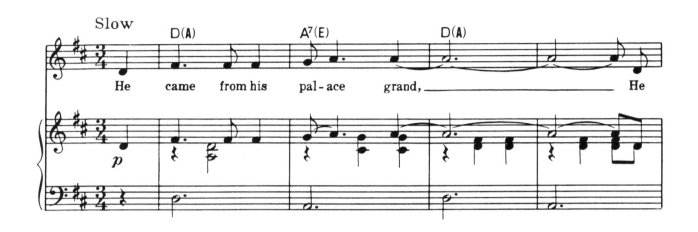

He came from his pal-ace grand, _____ He

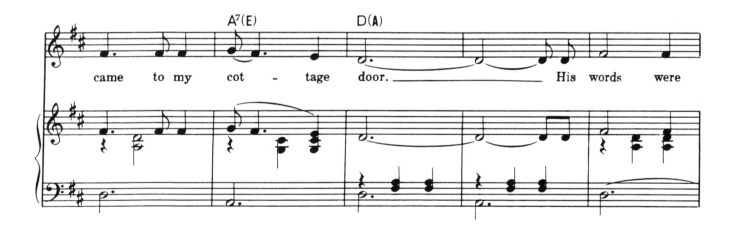

came to my cot - tage door. _____ His words were

few, but his looks _____ will lin-ger _____ for - ev - er - more _____

*As performed: A⁷(E).
**As performed: D(A).

2. There in her garden she stands,
    All dressed in fine satin and lace,
    Lady Mary so cold and so strange,
    Who finds in his heart no place.

    He knew I would be his bride,
    With a kiss for a lifetime fee,
    But I was nothing to him,
    And he was the world to me.

3. And now in his palace grand,
    On a flower strewn bed he lies,
    His beautiful lids are closed,
    O'er his sad dark beautiful eyes.

    And among the mourners who mourn,
    Why should I a mourner be?
    For I was nothing to him,
    And he was the world to me.

Originally part of a long Scots ballad, "Lord Jamie Douglas," all that remains are these few verses which constitute the emotional core of that ballad. Most singers know it in another form as "Waly, Waly," by which title it was known as far back as the early 18th century. It remains one of the most beautiful and evocative of all British lyric folksongs.

The Water is Wide

KEY: F   CAPO: 1ST   PLAY: E

Gently

The wat-er is wide, _____ I can-not get o'er, Neith-er have _____ I wings to_ fly. _____ Give me a boat _____ that can car-ry two, _____ and both shall cross, _____ my true love and I. _____

2.   I leaned my back against an oak,
Thinking it was a mighty tree,
But first it bent and then it broke,
So did my love prove false to me.

3.   I put my hand in some soft bush,
Thinking the sweetest flower to find,
I pricked my finger to the bone,
And left the sweetest flower behind.

4.   Oh, love is handsome and love is kind,
Gay as a jewel when it is new,
But love grows old and waxes cold,
And fades away like morning dew.

5.   The water is wide, I cannot get o'er, etc.

No more beautiful and simple folk lyric exists than the short verses of this piece. Known in various parts of the Southern Appalachians, its fame has been spread to the corners of the world in the fine versions of Jean Ritchie and John Jacob Niles. What many poets have taken hundreds of lines to say, the unknown folk composer of this song has been able to capsule in two short verses. The tune for this version is the work of John Jacob Niles.

Black is the Color

KEY: Eb MINOR   CAPO: NONE; GUITAR TUNED DOWN ½ TONE   PLAY: E MINOR

Moderately slow

Black, black, black ____ is the co - lor ____ of my true love's hair. His lips ____ are some - thing won - d'rous fair, ____ The

pur - - est eyes _____ and the brav - - - est _____

hands, _____ I love _____ the

ground _____ where - on _____ he _ stands. _____

Coda

Black, black, black _____ is the co - lor _____ of my

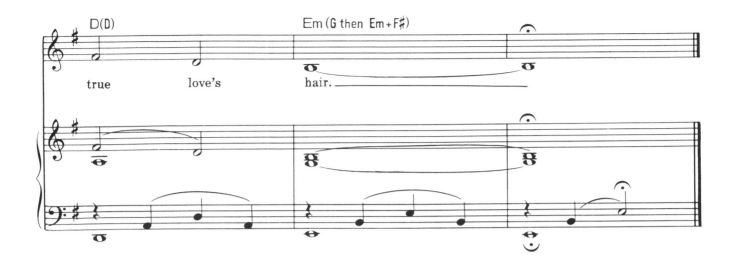

2. I love my love and well he knows,
I love the ground whereon he goes
And if my love no more I see,
My life would quickly fade away.

Black, black, black is the color of my true love's hair.

This is another lyric of frustrated love, several of its verses being traditionally found in combination with other lines. The dream verses (2 and 3) have the ring of art poetry to them, and may be a fairly recent accretion to the song.

Once I Had a Sweetheart

KEY: B♭   CAPO: 1ST   PLAY: A

Lively, lightly

Once I__ had a sweet-heart, and now__ I have none, Once I__ had a sweet-heart, and now__ I have none, He's gone__ and leave me, He's gone__ and leave me,

*As performed: A(G).

32

He's gone —— and leave me to sor - row and moan. 2. Last moan. ——

first and others

last

2. Last night in sweet slumber I dreamed I did see,
   Last night in sweet slumber I dreamed I did see,
   My own precious jewel sat smiling by me,
   My own precious jewel sat smiling by me.

3. And when I awakened I found it not so,
   And when I awakened I found it not so,
   My eyes like some fountain with tears overflow,
   My eyes like some fountain with tears overflow.

4. I'll venture through England, through France and through Spain,
   I'll venture through England, through France and through Spain,
   All my life I will venture the watery main,
   All my life I will venture the watery main.

5. Once I had a sweetheart, etc.

The refrain of this song is usually part of a British broadside ballad known in America as "Down By the Sea Shore" (Laws K 17). The verses, too, are, for the most part, widespread folk commonplaces. The unusual combination of the two, mainly the effort of Fred Hellerman, makes for an enchanting lyric on the theme of frustrated love.

I Never Will Marry

KEY: D   CAPO: NONE   PLAY: D

I nev-er will mar-ry, _____ I'll be no man's wife, _____ I in-tend to live sing-le _____ All the days of my life. _____

Some say that love is a gent-le thing, It on-ly has
brought me pain, _____ And the on-ly boy I e-ver
loved is gone on that mid-night train. _____

D.C. al Fine

*As performed: A⁷.

I never will marry, etc.   I never will marry, etc.

2. Your company, your company,   3. You'll see the grass whereon you stand
    Your company unto me,   Arise and grow again,
    It makes me feel while I'm away   But love it is a killin' thing,
    That every day is three.   Did you ever feel the pain?

                    I never will marry, etc.

4. I wish my heart were made of glass,
    Wherein you might behold,
    All the wonders of my love,
    The letters are writ in gold.

                    I never will marry, etc.

This lonesome song is known widely throughout the southern mountains, and is typical of the beautiful folk poetry which the mountaineers created to tell of heartbreak and sorrow, borrowing inspiration from older commonplace expressions found in British folk love songs. The tune is equally ubiquitous and adorns many other fine texts.

East Virginia

KEY: B MINOR   CAPO: 2ND   PLAY: A MINOR

2.   Her hair it was of a brightsome color,
And her lips of a ruby red,
On her breast she wore white lilies,
There I longed to lay my head.

3.   Well, in my heart you are my darlin',
At my door you're welcome in,
At my gate I'll meet you my darlin',
If your love I could only win.

4.   I'd rather be in some dark holler
Where the sun refused to shine,
Than to see you be another man's darlin',
And to know that you'll never be mine.

5.   Well in the night I'm dreamin' about you,
In the day I find no rest,
Just the thought of you my darlin',
Sends aching pains all through my breast.

6.   Well when I'm dead and in my coffin,
With my feet turned toward the sun,
Come and sit beside me darlin',
Come and think on the way you done.

This song was a favorite with broadside printers in England from the 17th century, and is still sung in parts of England and Scotland. The text sometimes runs to seven or more verses, but the two given here are fully representative of the rest.

I Once Loved a boy

KEY: E   CAPO: 4TH   PLAY: C

(C*) and (Em*) chords are to be played in higher position using first three strings.
**As performed: Gm(Dm). This and subsequent variations reflect implied harmonies of the guitar.

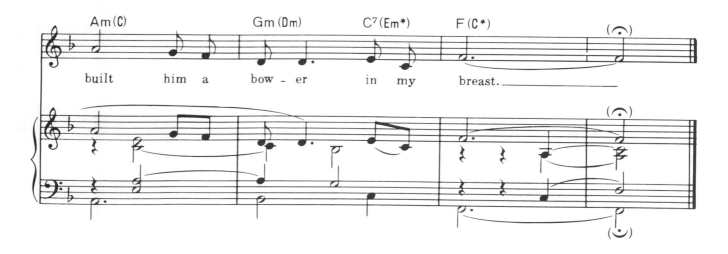

built him a bow - er in my breast._____

2. And this girl who has taken my bold bonnie lad,
   May she make of it all that she can,
   For whether he loves me or loves me not,
   I will walk with my love now and then.

The English collector Sabine Baring-Gould found this song in tradition in 1894 and believed it to date back to the period of the Stuart Restoration. Love metaphors utilizing playing cards motifs occur in the folksongs of many lands, but rarely as effectively as in this song.

KEY: F# MINOR   CAPO: 2ND   PLAY: E MINOR

2.   Had I the store in yonder mountain,
        Where gold and silver is there for countin'
        I could not count for thought of thee,
        My eyes so full I could not see.

3.   I love my father, I love my mother,
        I love my sister, I love my brother,
        I love my friends and relatives, too,
        I'll forsake them all and go with you.

4.   To the Queen of Hearts, etc.

Moderately

To the Queen of Hearts is the Ace of — Sor - row, he's here to - day, he's gone ——— to - mor - row, —— Young men are plen - ty but sweet-hearts —— few, If my love —— leaves me, —— what shall I do? ———

Pedal simile

first and others   *last*

This is a variant text of one of the most beautiful of all lyric songs of British origin. Robert Burns knew a folk version which he revised with a sure touch, but the folk preferred their own versions, and have kept the song in living tradition for several hundred years. The music for this version is the work of David Gude of Martha's Vineyard.

Fare Thee Well
(TEN THOUSAND MILES)

KEY: F#   CAPO: 4TH   PLAY: D

*As performed: G(D).

**As performed: Em(Bm) throughout this section.

2. Oh, ten thousand miles it is so far to leave me here alone,
While I may lie, lament and cry, and you, you'll not hear my moan,
And you'll,———no you'll, and you'll not hear my moan.

3. Oh, the crow that is so black my love will change his color white,
If ever I should prove false to thee, the day, day will turn to night,
Yes, the day,———oh the day, yes the day will turn to night.

4. Oh, the rivers never will run dry, or the rocks melt with the sun,
I'll never prove false to the boy I love, 'til all, all these things be done,
'Til all,———'til all, 'til all these things be done.

This incomparable lyric lament on false suitors is perhaps the best known of all such pieces from the Southern Appalachians. Numerous textual variants are known, sung to almost as many different tunes. Some of its verses can be traced back to British songs, while others are found only in America. Taken together they form an exquisite example of lyric folk song.

Come All Ye Fair and Tender Maidens

KEY: F   CAPO: 3RD   PLAY: D

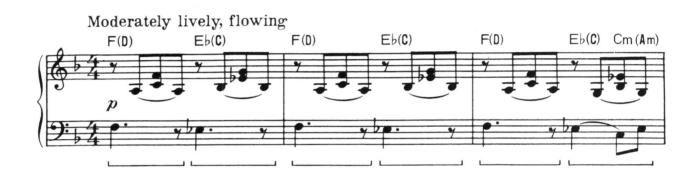

Come all ye fair _____

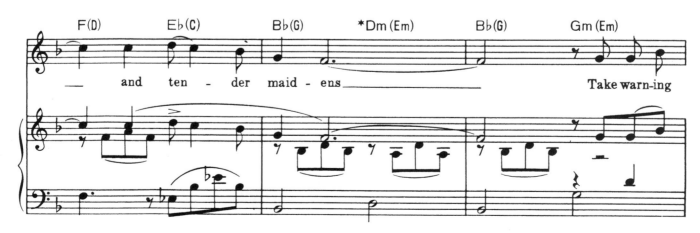

____ and ten - der maid - ens _____   Take warn-ing

*As performed: Gm(Em).

how _____ you court young men, _____

They're like a _ star _____ of a sum-mer's

morn-ing, _____ First they'll ap-pear, _____ and then they're

gone. _____

first and others

last

45

2. They'll tell to you some lovin' story,
   They'll swear to you their love is true,
   Straight-way they'll go and court another,
   And that's the love they had for you.

3. Oh, do you remember our days of courtin'
   When your head lay upon my breast?
   You could make me believe
           with the fallin' of your arm
   That the sun rose in the West.

4. If I'd a known before I courted
   That love it was such a killin' thing,
   I'd a locked my heart in a box of golden
   And fastened it up with a silver pin.

5. I wish I was a little sparrow,
   And I had wings and I could fly,
   I'd fly away to my own true lover,
   And when he'd speak I would deny.

6. But I am not no little sparrow,
   I have no wings, neither can I fly,
   I'll sit right down in my grief and sorrow,
   And let my troubles pass me by.

7. Come all ye fair and tender maidens, etc.

CHILD BALLADS

Among the finest of all the folksongs in the English-speaking world are the 305 classic British ballads which Francis James Child of Harvard recognized as being truly traditional, and which he analyzed in great detail in his monumental five volume work, The English and Scottish Popular Ballads *(1882-1898). These ballads are still identified by the numbers which he assigned to them and, though more than half a century has passed since his work was completed, only a few ballads have been recommended as additions to Child's canon, an indication of the degree to which Child's selections have become the standard by which all balladry is judged.*

Geordie

An 18th century English broadside ballad has intertwined with a 17th century traditional Scottish ballad to produce one of the dramatic gems of British balladry. Poaching, even by a nobleman, was a serious crime. His high position, however, entitled him to a death befitting his station in life. Geordie's sweetheart (or wife) pleads for his life, usually to no avail, though in at least one other version he obtains his freedom thanks to the sheer force of her character.

KEY: F MINOR   CAPO: 1ST   PLAY: E MINOR   (CHILD NO. 209)

*As performed: E(D).
**As performed: F#m(Em).

48

2.   Ah, my Geordie will be hanged in a golden chain
      'Tis not the chain of many
      He was born of king's royal breed
      And lost to a virtuous lady.

3.   Go bridle me my milk white steed,
      Go bridle me my pony,
      I will ride to London's court
      To plead for the life of Geordie.

4.   Ah, my Geordie never stole nor cow nor calf,
      He never hurted any,
      Stole sixteen of the king's royal deer,
      And he sold them in Bohenny.

5.   Two pretty babies have I born,
      The third lies in my body,
      I'd freely part with them every one
      If you'd spare the life of Geordie.

6.   The judge looked over his left shoulder,
      He said fair maid I'm sorry
      He said fair maid you must be gone,
      For I cannot pardon Geordie.

7.   Ah, my Geordie will be hanged in a golden chain,
      'Tis not the chain of many,
      Stole sixteen of the king's royal deer
      And he sold them in Bohenny.

49

This may well be but one half of a longer ballad in which a sinking of a merchant ship by a pirate is revenged when the King sends one of his captains to locate, defeat and capture the pirate. As given here, we have the first half of that tale; the rest of the story is dramatically told in another Child ballad, "Sir Andrew Barton" (Child No. 167). Both ballads have been collected frequently from traditional singers in America.

Henry Martin

KEY: B MINOR   CAPO: 2ND   PLAY: A MINOR   (CHILD NO. 250)

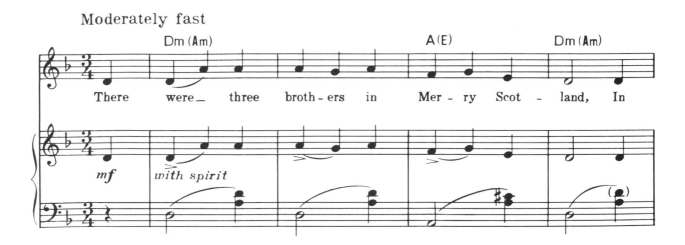

Moderately fast

Dm (Am)   A (E)   Dm (Am)

There were— three broth-ers in Mer - ry Scot - land, In

mf   with spirit

2.   The lot it fell first upon Henry Martin,
The youngest of all the three,
That he should turn robber all on the salt sea, the salt sea, the salt sea,
For to maintain his two brothers and he.

3.   They had not been sailing but a long Winter's night,
And part of a short Winter's day,
When he espied a stout lofty ship, lofty ship, lofty ship
Come a-bibbing down on him straight way.

4.   "Hello, hello," cried Henry Martin
"What makes you sail so nigh?"
"I'm a rich merchant ship bound for fair London town, London town,
    London town,
Would you please for to let me pass by?"

5.   "Oh, no, oh no," cried Henry Martin,
"This thing it never could be,
For I have turned robber all on the salt sea, the salt sea, the salt sea,
For to maintain my two brothers and me."

6.   "Come lower your tops'l and brail up your mizzen,
Bring your ship under my lee
Or I will give to you a full cannon ball, cannon ball, cannon ball,
And all your dear bodies drown in the salt sea."

7.   "Oh no, we won't lower our lofty topsail,
Nor bring our ship under your lee
And you shan't take from us our rich merchant goods, merchant
    goods, merchant goods,
Nor point our bold guns to the sea.

8.   And broadside and broadside and at it they went
For fully two hours or three,
'Til Henry Martin gave to them the death shot, the death shot,
    the death shot
And straight to the bottom went she.

9.   Bad news, bad news to old England came,
Bad news to fair London town,
There's been a rich vessel and she's cast away, cast away, cast away,
And all of her merry men drowned.

Mary Hamilton

The ballad tale told here bears resemblance to two distinct historical occurrences: one relating to a 16th century incident in the court of Mary Queen of Scots, and the other to an affair in the court of Russia's Czar Peter in the 18th century. At this late date, however, oral tradition has altered the story too greatly to pinpoint the exact incident on which the ballad might have been based. The long circumstantial version given here does not have much currency today among traditional singers; all that usually remains is a lyric lament in which Mary Hamilton makes a farewell speech without any explanation of why she is being punished.

KEY: B   CAPO: 2ND   PLAY: A   (CHILD NO. 173)

Quite moderately

Word is to the kit-chen gone And word is to the hall, And word is up to Mad-am the Queen And that's the worst of all,

2.   "Arise, arise, Mary Hamilton,
      Arise and tell to me,
      What thou hast done with thy wee babe
      I saw and heard weep by thee?"

3.   "I put him in a tiny boat,
      And cast him out to sea,
      That he might sink or he might swim,
      But he'd never come back to me."

4.   "Arise, arise, Mary Hamilton,
      Arise and come with me;
      There is a wedding in Glasgow town,
      This night we'll go and see."

5.   She put not on her robes of black,
      Nor her robes of brown,
      But she put on her robes of white,
      To ride into Glasgow town.

6.   And as she rode into Glasgow town,
      The city for to see,
      The bailiff's wife and the provost's wife
      Cried, "Ach, and alas for thee."

7.   "Ah, you need not weep for me," she cried,
      "You need not weep for me;
      For had I not slain my own wee babe,
      This death I would not dee."

8..   "Ah, little did my mother think
      When first she cradled me,
      The lands I was to travel in,
      And the death I was to dee."

9.   "Last night I washed the Queen's feet,
      And put the gold in her hair,
      And the only reward I find for this,
      The gallows to be my share."

10.   "Cast off, cast off my gown," she cried,
      "But let my petticoat be,
      And tie a napkin 'round my face;
      The gallows I would not see."

11.   Then by and come the King himself,
      Looked up with a pitiful eye,
      "Come down, come down, Mary Hamilton,
      Tonight, you'll dine with me."

12.   "Ah, hold your tongue, my sovereign liege,
      And let your folly be;
      For if you'd a mind to save my life,
      You'd never have shamed me here."

13.   "Last night there were four Marys,
      Tonight there'll be but three,
      There was Mary Beaton, and Mary Seton,
      And Mary Carmichael, and me."

Silkie

"The Great Silkie of Sule Skerry" is one of numerous tales of the 'Silkies,' or sealfolk, known to the inhabitants of the Orkney Islands and the Hebrides. These enchanted creatures dwell in the depth of the sea, occasionally doffing their seal skins to pass on land as mortal men. Legend has it that they then accept human partners, and some families on the islands actually trace their ancestry to such marriages. In more complete versions of the ballad the Silkie's forecast of the death of himself and his son (stanzas 5 and 6) eventually come to pass. The tune is by Dr. James Waters of Columbia University.

KEY: D   CAPO: NONE   PLAY: D   (CHILD NO. 113)

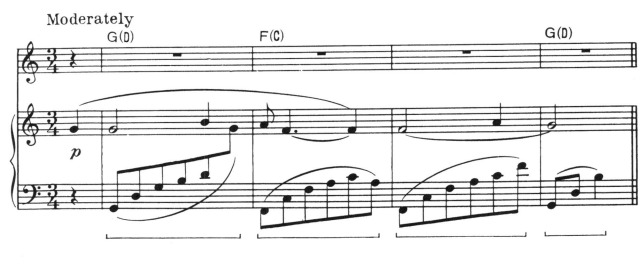

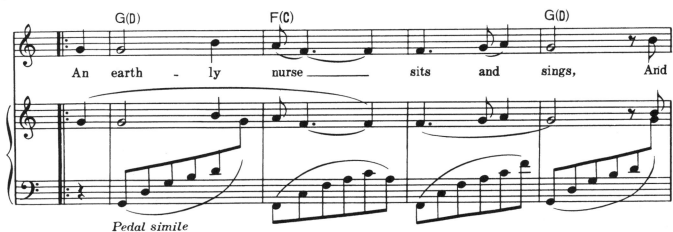

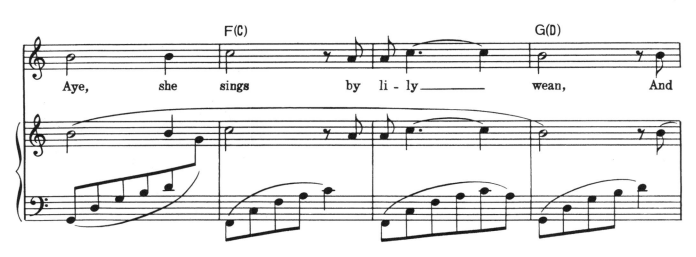

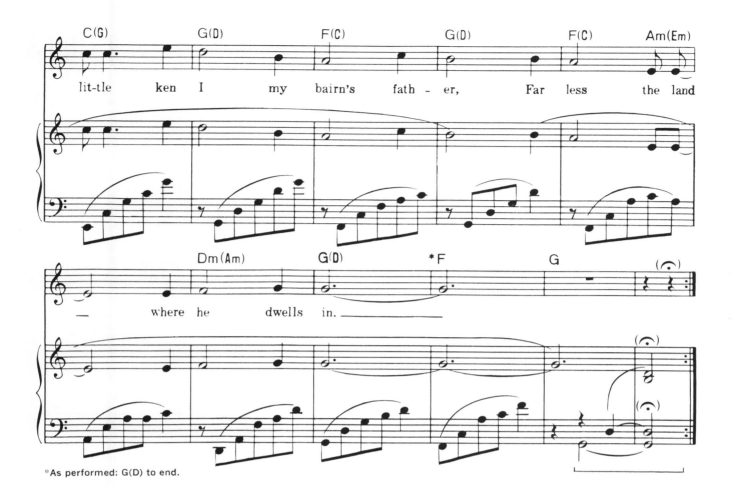

lit-tle ken I my bairn's fath - er, Far less the land
— where he dwells in.

*As performed: G(D) to end.

2. For he came one night to her bed feet,
   And a grumbly guest, I'm sure was he,
   Saying "Here am I, thy bairn's father,
   Although I be not comely."

3. "I am a man upon the land,
   I am a silkie on the sea,
   And when I'm far and far frae land,
   My home it is in Sule Skerrie."

4. And he had ta'en a purse of gold
   And he had placed it upon her knee,
   Saying, "Give to me my little young son,
   And take thee up thy nurse's feē."

5. "And it shall come to pass on a summer's day,
   When the sun shines bright on every stane,
   I'll come and fetch my little young son,
   And teach him how to swim the faem."

6. "And ye shall marry a gunner good,
   And a right fine gunner I'm sure he'll be,
   And the very first shot that e'er he shoots
   Will kill both my young son and me."

This is without doubt the best known and most widely sung of all British traditional ballads, both in the Old World and in America. Most variants strongly resemble one another, undoubtedly due to the frequent publication of this ballad in songsters, chapbooks, penny garlands and on broadsides from the 17th century on.

Barbara Allen

KEY: B   CAPO: 2ND   PLAY: A   (CHILD NO. 84)

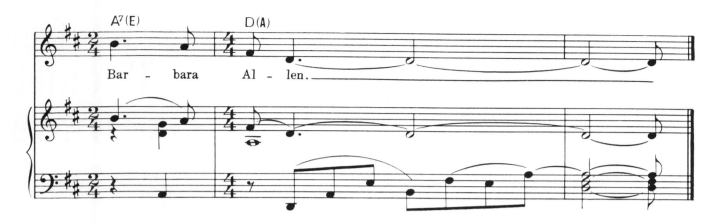

2. He sent his servant to the town,
   To the place where she was dwellin',
   Saying, "You must come to my master dear,
   If your name be Barb'ry Allen."

3. So, slowly, slowly she got up,
   And slowly she drew nigh him,
   And the only words to him did say,
   "Young man, I think you're dyin'."

4. He turned his face unto the wall,
   And death was in him wellin',
   "Good-bye, good-bye to my friends all,
   Be good to Barb'ry Allen."

5. When he was dead and laid in grave,
   She heard the death bells knellin',
   And every stroke to her did say:
   "Hard-hearted Barb'ry Allen."

6. "Oh mother, oh mother, go dig my grave,
   Make it both long and narrow;
   Sweet William died of love for me,
   And I will die of sorrow."

7. "And father, oh father, go dig my grave,
   Make it both long and narrow,
   Sweet William died on yesterday,
   And I will die tomorrow."

8. Barb'ry Allen was buried in the old church-yard,
   Sweet William was buried beside her;
   Out of Sweet William's heart there grew a rose,
   Out of Barb'ry Allen's, a briar.

9. They grew and grew in the old church-yard,
   'Til they could grow no higher;
   At the end they formed a true lovers' knot,
   And the rose grew 'round the briar.

Aside from its exquisite poetry and music, this ballad is notable for its exhibition of the universal popular belief that excessive grief on the part of mourners disturbs the peace of the dead. Most of the verses of "The Unquiet Grave" can be found in other ballads and folk lyrics, suggesting the possibility that what we have here is only a fragment of a longer ballad still undiscovered. But in its few short verses it presents a compelling and highly dramatic vignette of love, death and grief.

The Unquiet Grave

KEY: C   CAPO: NONE   PLAY: C   (CHILD NO. 78)

Cold blows the wind to my true love, And gent - ly drops the rain.

*As performed: C.
**As performed: G⁷ throughout.

60

2. I'll do as much for my true love,
   As any young girl may,
   I'll sit and mourn all on his grave,
   For twelve months and a day.

3. And when twelve months and a day was passed,
   The ghost did rise and speak,
   "Why sittest thou all on my grave
   And will not let me sleep?"

4. "Go fetch me water from the desert,
   And blood from out the stone,
   Go fetch me milk from a fair maid's breast
   That young man never has known."

5. "My breast it is as cold as clay,
   My breath is earthly strong,
   And if you kiss my cold clay lips
   Your days they won't be long."

6. "How oft on yonder grave, sweetheart,
   Where we were wont to walk,
   The fairest flower that e'er I saw
   Has withered to a stalk."

7. "When will we meet again, sweetheart,
   When will we meet again?"
   "When the Autumn leaves that fall from the trees
   Are green and spring up again."

This is one of the most popular of English religious folk ballads. Its tale derives from the Pseudo-Matthew gospel, and in medieval times was frequently dramatized in folk plays and mystery pageants including, among others, those performed by the Grey Friars in Coventry. Fuller versions of the ballad sometimes contain predictions of Jesus' birth, death and resurrection.

The Cherry Tree Carol

KEY: D   CAPO: NONE; TUNE 6TH STRING TO D   PLAY: D   (CHILD NO. 54)

*As performed: B♭(G).

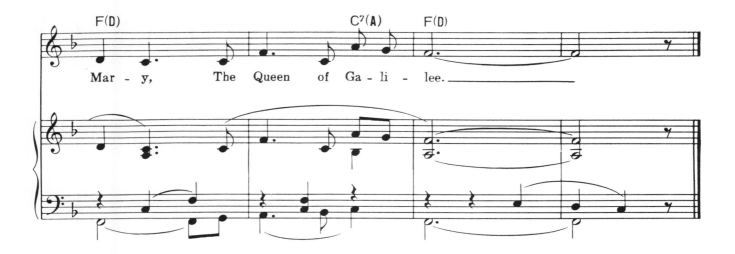

Mar - y, The Queen of Ga - li - lee. _____

2. Joseph and Mary walked through an orchard green,
There were berries and cherries as thick as might be seen,
There were berries and cherries as thick as might be seen.

3. And Mary spoke to Joseph, so meek and so mild,
"Joseph gather me some cherries, for I am with child,
Joseph gather me some cherries, for I am with child."

4. And Joseph flew in anger, in anger flew he,
"Let the father of the baby gather cherries for thee,
Let the father of the baby gather cherries for thee."

5. Then up spoke baby Jesus from in Mary's womb,
"Bend down the tallest tree that my mother might have some,
Bend down the tallest tree that my mother might have some."

6. And bent down the tallest branch 'til it touched Mary's hand,
Cried she, "Oh, look thou Joseph, I have cherries by command,"
Cried she, "Oh, look thou Joseph, I have cherries by command."

Lady Gay

This is one of the best of the American versions of "The Wife of Usher's Well," a remarkable ballad on the theme of persistent grief and tears disturbing the sleep of the dead. The children have been sent away to learn magic (grammaree), a point rarely recognized by the folk who sing the ballad. The children's death and their mother's prayer for their return culminates in their ghostly visit to warn her of the effect of her mourning. In most American versions of the Child ballads supernatural motifs disappear, except where, as in the case of "Lady Gay," there are religious overtones to the ballad tale.

KEY: Eb   CAPO: 3RD   PLAY: C   (CHILD NO. 79)

There was a La - dy and a La - dy Gay, ____ Of _ child - ren she had three, ____ She sent them a - way ____ to the North Coun - tree ____ To learn their

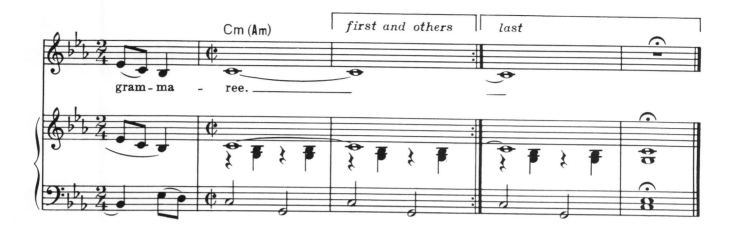

gram - ma - ree. _____

2. They'd not been gone but a very short time,
    Scarcely three weeks and a day,
    When death, cruel death, came harkening along
    And stole those babes away.

3. "There is a King in Heaven", she cried,
    "A King of third degree
    Send back, send back my three little babes,
    This night send them back to me."

4. She made a bed in the uppermost room,
    On it she put a white sheet,
    And over the top a golden spread
    That they much better might sleep.

5. "Take it off, take it off," cried the older one,
    "Take it off, take it off," cried he,
    "For what's to become
        of this wide wicked world
    Since sin has first begun."

6. She set a table of linen fine,
    On it she placed bread and wine,
    "Come eat, come drink, my three little babes
    Come eat, come drink of mine."

7. "We want none of your bread, mother,
    Neither do we want your wine,
    For yonder stands our Savior dear,
    To Him we must resign."

8. "Green grass is over our heads, mother,
    Cold clay is over our feet,
    And every tear you shed for us,
    It wets our winding-sheet."

65

Child's title for this ballad, "James Harris, or the Daemon Lover," indicates the supernatural status of the returning lover, a point which is usually rationalized or eliminated in most American versions. In this fine version, however, the demonic character of the suitor is alluded to in the dramatic closing verses. Next to "Barbara Allen," this is probably the most popular of the Child ballads performed in American tradition.

House Carpenter

KEY: C MINOR   CAPO: 3RD   PLAY: A MINOR   (CHILD NO. 243)

*As performed: Dm(Am).

2. "I could have married the king's daughter, dear,
   She would have married me,
   But I have forsaken her crowns of gold
   All for the love of thee."

3. "Well, if you could have married the king's
   daughter, dear,
   I'm sure you are to blame,
   For I am married to a house carpenter,
   I find him a nice young man."

4. "Ah, will you forsake your house carpenter,
   And go along with me,
   I'll take you where the grass grows green,
   By the banks of the salt, salt sea."

5. "Well, if I should forsake my house carpenter,
   And go along with thee,
   What have you got to maintain me on
   And keep me from poverty."

6. "Six ships, six ships all out on the sea,
   Seven more upon dry land,
   One hundred and ten all brave sailor men,
   Will be at your command."

7. She picked up her own wee babe,
   And kisses gave him three,
   Said, "Stay right here with my house carpenter,
   And keep him good company."

8. Then she putted on her rich attire,
   So glorious to behold,
   And as she trod along her way,
   She shone like the glittering gold.

9. Well they'd not been gone but about
   two weeks,
   I know it was not three,
   When this fair lady began to weep,
   She wept most bitterly.

10. "Ah, why do you weep, my fair young maid,
    Weep you for your golden store
    Or do you weep for your house carpenter,
    Who never you shall see any more."

11. "I do not weep for my house carpenter
    Or for any golden store,
    I do weep for my own wee babe
    Who never I shall see any more."

12. Well, they'd not been gone but
    about three weeks,
    I'm sure it was not four,
    Our gallant ship sprang a leak and sank,
    Never to rise any more.

13. One time 'round spun our gallant ship
    Two times 'round spun she,
    Three times around spun our gallant ship
    And sank to the bottom of the sea.

14. "What hills, what hills are those, my love,
    That rise so fair and high?"
    "Those are the hills of Heaven my love,
    But not for you and I."

15. "And what hills, what hills are those,
    my love,
    Those hills so dark and low?"
    "Those are the hills of Hell, my love,
    Where you and I must go."

This dramatic ballad traces back to at least the beginning of the 17th century in Britain, but has proven more popular in this country than in the Old World. Its tale of adultery and the gruesome revenge which follows has struck a responsive note in the New World wherever Puritan and Calvinist precepts hold sway, undoubtedly accounting for its widespread popularity in this country despite its great length.

Matty Groves

KEY: Bb MINOR   CAPO: 1ST   PLAY: A MINOR   (CHILD NO. 81)

Moderately and freely

*As performed: Bm(Am), F#(E).
**For some verses: Em(Dm) passing through Bm(Am) and F#(E) to Bm(Am).

2.   He spied three ladies dressed in black,
As they came into view,
Lord Arlen's wife was gaily clad,
A flower among the few, a flower among the few.

3.   She trippèd up to Matty Groves,
Her eyes so low cast down,
Saying, "Pray, oh, pray come with me stay,
As you pass through the town, as you pass through the town."

4.   "I cannot go, I dare not go,
I fear 'twould cost my life,
For I see by the little ring you wear,
You are Lord Arlen's wife, you're the great Lord Arlen's wife."

5.   "This may be false, this may be true,
I can't deny it all,
Lord Arlen's gone to consecrate
King Henry at Whitehall, King Henry at Whitehall."

6.   "Oh, pray, oh pray come with me stay,
I'll hide thee out of sight,
I'll serve you there beyond compare,
And sleep with you the night, and sleep with you the night."

7.   Her little page did listen well,
To all that they did say,
And ere the sun could rise again
He quickly sped away, he quickly sped away.

8.   And he did run the Kings' highway,
He swam across the tide,
He ne'er did stop until he came
To the great Lord Arlen's side, to the great Lord Arlen's side.

9.   "What news, what news, my bully boy,
What news brings you to me,
My castle burned, my tenants robbed,
My lady with baby, my lady with baby?"

10.   "No harm has come your house and land,"
The little page did say,
"But Matty Groves is bedded up
With your fair lady gay, with your fair lady gay."

11.   Lord Arlen called his merry men,
He bade them with him go,
He bade them ne'er a word to speak,
And ne'er a horn to blow, and ne'er a horn to blow.

12. But among Lord Arlen's merry men
    Was one who wished no ill,
    And the bravest lad in all the crew
    Blew his horn so loud and shrill, blew his horn so loud and shrill.

13. "What's this, what's this," cried Matty Groves,
    "What's this that I do hear?
    It must be Lord Arlen's merry men,
    The ones that I do fear, the ones that I do fear."

14. "Lie down, lie down, little Matty Groves,
    And keep my back from cold,
    It's only Lord Arlen's merry men
    A-callin' the sheep to fold, a-callin' the sheep to fold."

15. Little Matty Groves he did lie down,
    He took a nap asleep,
    And when he woke Lord Arlen was
    A-standing at his feet, a-standing at his feet.

16. "How now, how now, my bully boy,
    And how do you like my sheets?
    And how do you like my fair young bride
    Who lies in your arms asleep, who lies in your arms asleep?"

17. "Ah, it's very well I like your bed,
    And it's fine I like your sheets,
    But it's best I like your fair young bride
    Who lies in my arms asleep, who lies in my arms asleep."

18. "Rise up, rise up, little Matty Groves,
    As fast as e'er you can;
    In England it shall ne'er be said
    I slew a sleeping man, I slew a sleeping man."

19. And the firstest stroke little Matty struck,
    He hurt Lord Arlen sore,
    But the nextest stroke Lord Arlen struck,
    Little Matty struck no more, little Matty struck no more.

20. "Rise up, rise up, my gay young bride,
    Draw on your pretty clothes,
    Now tell me do you like me best
    Or like you Matty Groves, or the dying Matty Groves?"

21. She picked up Matty's dying head,
    She kissed from cheek to chin,
    Said, "It's Matty Groves I'd rather have
    Than Arlen and all his kin, than Arlen and all his kin."

22. "Ah, woe is me and woe is thee,
    Why stayed you not your hand?
    For you have killed the fairest lad
    In all of England, in all of England."

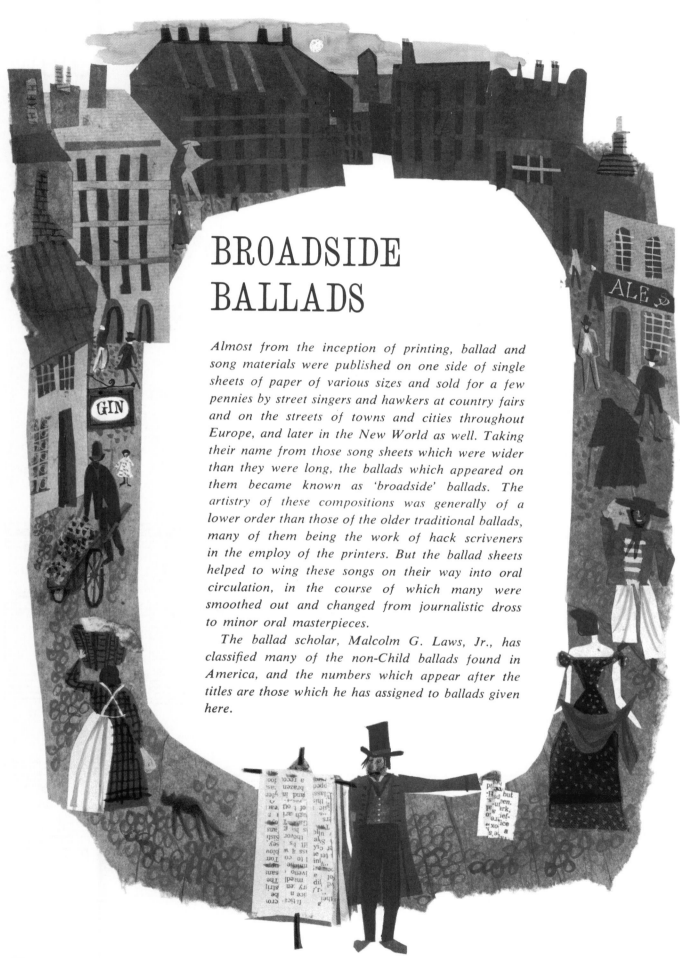

BROADSIDE BALLADS

Almost from the inception of printing, ballad and song materials were published on one side of single sheets of paper of various sizes and sold for a few pennies by street singers and hawkers at country fairs and on the streets of towns and cities throughout Europe, and later in the New World as well. Taking their name from those song sheets which were wider than they were long, the ballads which appeared on them became known as 'broadside' ballads. The artistry of these compositions was generally of a lower order than those of the older traditional ballads, many of them being the work of hack scriveners in the employ of the printers. But the ballad sheets helped to wing these songs on their way into oral circulation, in the course of which many were smoothed out and changed from journalistic dross to minor oral masterpieces.

The ballad scholar, Malcolm G. Laws, Jr., has classified many of the non-Child ballads found in America, and the numbers which appear after the titles are those which he has assigned to ballads given here.

The rejected suitor who in turn rejects his false lover when she finally calls for him is a popular theme in traditional and broadside balladry, and numerous different versifications have been collected from traditional singers on both sides of the Atlantic Ocean. This is one of the best of them, uncomplicated by the introduction of other themes.

Once I Knew a Pretty Girl

KEY: E MINOR   CAPO: NONE   PLAY: E MINOR   (LAWS P 10)

Slow and very free

1. Once I knew a pret-ty girl ___ I loved her as my life ___ I'd

glad - ly give my heart and hand ___ to make her ___ my

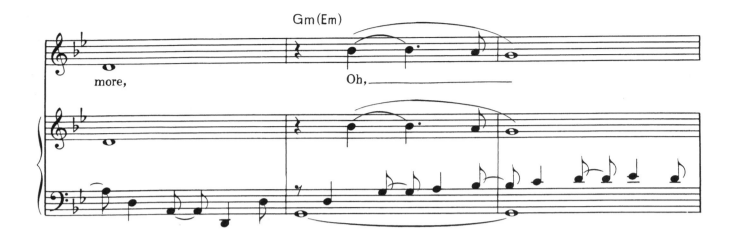

more,   Oh, _____

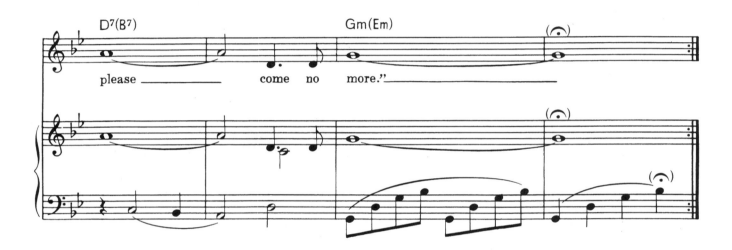

please _____ come no more." _____

3. Well, I'd not been gone but about six months,
When she did complain,
And she wrote me a letter,
Saying, "Please come back again,
Ooh, please come again."

4. And I wrote her an answer,
Just for to let her know,
That no young man should venture,
Where once he could not go,
Ooh, where once he could not go.

5. So come all ye young lovers,
Take a warning from me,
And never place your affections
On a green growin' tree,
Ooh, on a green growin' tree.

6. 'Cause the leaves they will wither,
Roots will decay,
And the beauty of a young maid,
Will soon fade away,
Ooh, soon fade away.

Silver Dagger

Family opposition to the marriage of lovers takes many forms in traditional ballads, almost all of which end either with the lovers committing suicide or one of them being done away with by the recalcitrant parents. In this version of "The Silver Dagger," however, the ballad ends inconclusively for we are not told what course will be taken by the rejected lover.

KEY: Db   CAPO: 4TH   PLAY: A   (LAWS M 4 AND G 21)

2. All men are false, says my mother,
They'll tell you wicked, lovin' lies.
The very next evening, they'll court another,
Leave you alone to pine and sigh.

3. My daddy is a handsome devil,
He's got a chain five miles long,
And on every link a heart does dangle
Of another maid he's loved and wronged.

4. Go court another tender maiden,
And hope that she will be your wife,
For I've been warned, and I've decided
To sleep alone all of my life.

This ballad appears to have been founded on an actual occurrence. In the 17th century, young Lord Craigton was married to Elizabeth Innes, a girl several years his senior, in a child marriage intended to consolidate family fortunes. The young husband died several years later. The use of a colored ribbon as a marriage token (stanza 4) is a centuries-old tradition still found in rural folk communities. The ballad is widely known in Scotland ("Lang A-Growing"), Ireland ("The Bonny Boy"), and in England under the title given here.

The Trees They Do Grow High

KEY: F MINOR   CAPO: 1ST   PLAY: E MINOR   (LAWS O 35)

Moderately slow

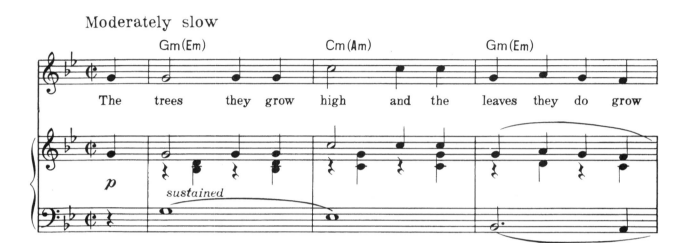

The trees they grow high and the leaves they do grow

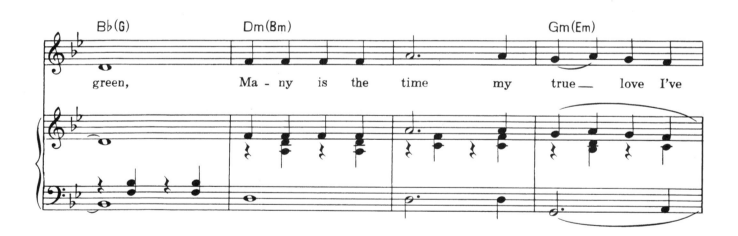

green, Ma-ny is the time my true—love I've

seen, Ma-ny an hour I've watched him all a-lone, He's

*As performed: Gm(Em).

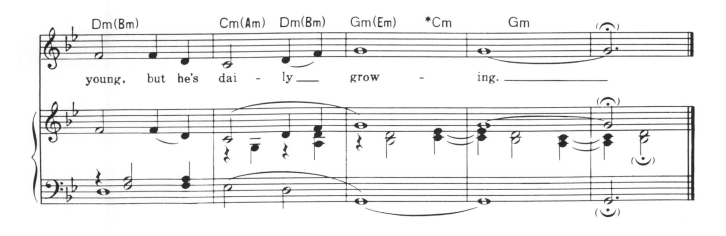

young, but he's dai - ly — grow - ing. —

2.   Father, dear father, you've done me great wrong,
You have married me to a boy who is too young,
I'm twice twelve and he is but fourteen,
He's young but he's daily growing.

3.   Daughter, dear daughter, I've done you no wrong,
I have married you to a great lord's son,
He'll make a lord for you to wait upon,
He's young but he's daily growing.

4.   Father, dear father, if you see fit,
We'll send him to college for one year yet,
I'll tie blue ribbons all around his head,
To let the maidens know that he's married.

5.   One day I was lookin' o'er my father's castle wall,
I spied all the boys a-playin' with the ball,
My own true love was the flower of them all,
He's young but he's daily growing.

6.   At the age of fourteen, he was a married man,
At the age of fifteen, the father of a son,
At the age of sixteen, his grave it was green,
And death had put an end to his growing.

The girl who disguises herself as a soldier or sailor in order to be at the side of her lover is an age-old theme, and in English alone more than 20 different ballads on this theme have been collected from traditional singers. "Jackaroe" is one of the most popular of these to be found in America. Here, as in most ballads about a "female warrior," all ends well.

Jackaroe

KEY: D MINOR   CAPO: 5TH   PLAY: A MINOR   (LAWS N 7)

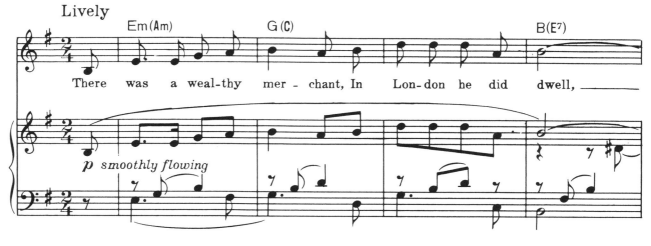

There was a weal-thy mer-chant, In Lon-don he did dwell, _____

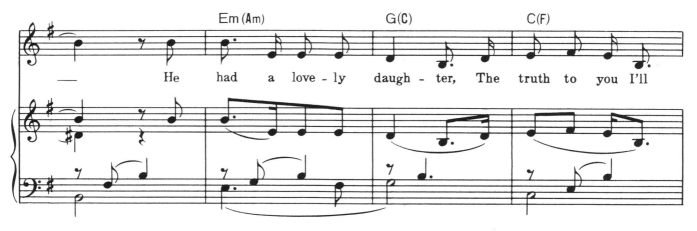

— He had a love-ly daugh-ter, The truth to you I'll

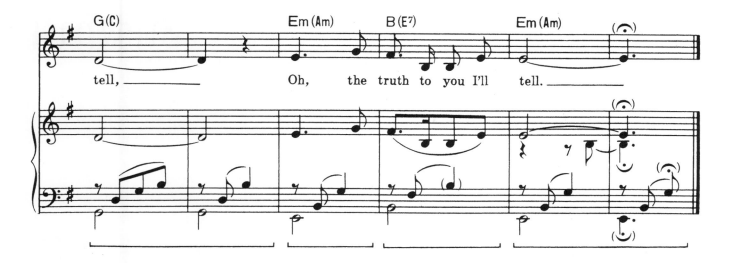

tell, _____ Oh, the truth to you I'll tell. _____

2. She had sweethearts a-plenty and men of high degree,
There was none but Jack the sailor her true love e'er could be,
Oh, her true love e'er could be.

3. Now Jackie's gone a-sailing with trouble on his mind,
To leave his native country and his darling girl behind,
Oh, his darling girl behind.

4. She went into a tailor shop and dressed in men's array,
And stepped on board a vessel to convey herself away,
Oh, convey herself away.

5. "Before you step on board, sir, your name I'd like to know."
She smiled all in her countenance, "they call me Jackaroe,
Oh, they call me Jackaroe."

6. "Your waist is light and slender, your fingers are neat and small
Your cheeks too red and rosy to face the cannon-ball,
Oh, to face the cannon-ball."

7. "I know my waist is slender, my fingers neat and small,
But it would not make me tremble to see ten thousand fall,
Oh, to see ten thousand fall."

8. The war soon being over, they hunted all around,
And among the dead and dying her darling boy she found,
Oh, her darling boy she found.

9. She picked him up all in her arms and carried him to the town,
And sent for a physician who quickly healed his wounds,
Oh, who quickly healed his wounds.

10. This couple, they got married, so well did they agree,
This couple they got married, so why not you and me,
Oh, so why not you and me.

Stewball

In its original Irish form, this ballad told of a race between a horse named 'Sku-ball' and a mare, 'Miss Portly,' on the Kildare race track in the early 19th century. In America the song has been most popular in the Negro south, where the winning horse is known variously as 'Stewball' or 'Kimball.' The music for this version is the work of the Greenbriar Boys.

KEY: C   CAPO: NONE   PLAY: C   (LAWS Q 22)

Lazy rhythm

Stew-ball was a good horse, _____ He wore a high

head, _____ And the mane on his fore-top _____

(small notes optional for any verse)

_____ Was as fine as silk thread. _____

2.   I rode him in England,
       I rode him in Spain,
       And I never did lose, boys,
       I always did gain.

3.   So come all you gamblers,
       Wherever you are,
       And don't bet your money
       On that little gray mare.

4.   Most likely she'll stumble,
       Most likely she'll fall,
       But you never will lose, boys,
       On my noble Stewball.

5.   As they were a-ridin'
       'Bout halfway around,
       That gray mare she stumbled
       And fell on the ground.

6.   And away out yonder,
       Ahead of them all,
       Came a-prancin' an' dancin'
       My noble Stewball.

The original British broadside ballad from which this version is descended lists the many crimes of the narrator, including the robbery of various Lords, Dukes and Earls, for which he is eventually condemned to the gallows. In oral tradition the narrative element is pretty weak, his crimes are generalized and his burial instructions give no indication of his capture and sentencing. Its handsome tune more than makes up for the loss of details in this ballad version.

Rake and Rambling Boy

KEY: C   CAPO: 3RD   PLAY: A   (LAWS L 12)

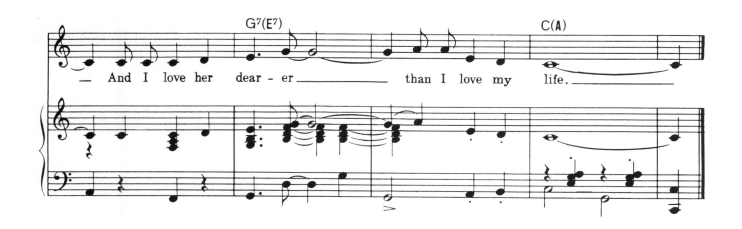

2. Oh, she was pretty, both neat and gay,
   Caused me to rob the broad highway,
   Oh, yes I robbed it, I do declare,
   And I got myself ten thousand there.

3. Well, I'm a rake, etc.

4. Oh, when I die, don't bury me at all,
   Place my bones in alcohol,
   And at my feet, place a white snow dove,
   To tell the world that I died for love.

5. Well, I'm a rake, etc.

Fennario

Cecil Sharp discovered several versions of this ballad in the Southern Appalachians on his collecting trips during the first World War, though it appears to have disappeared from American tradition since that time. It is still extremely popular in Scotland as "The Bonnie Lass o' Fyvie—O" and was earlier known in England as "Pretty Peggy of Derby."

KEY: E   CAPO: 4TH   PLAY: C

Moderately lively

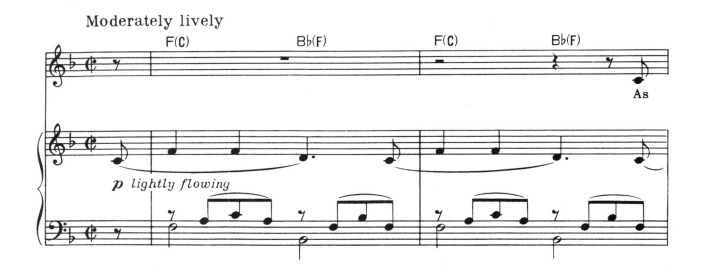

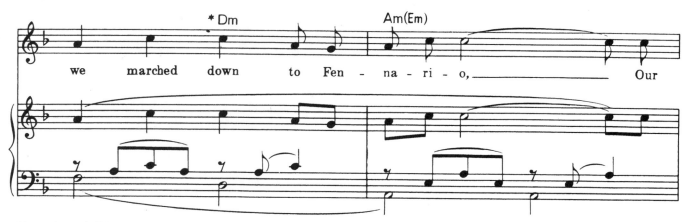

*As performed: F(C).

*As performed: C(G).
**As performed: F(C) is retained.
***As performed: Bb(F) is retained.

2.   What will your mother think, pretty Peggy, oh?
        What will your mother think, pretty Peggy, oh?
        What will your mother think, when she hears the guineas clink,
        And the soldiers all marching before you, oh?

3. In a carriage you will ride, pretty Peggy, oh,
In a carriage you will ride, pretty Peggy, oh,
In a carriage you will ride, with your true love by your side
As fair as any maiden in the areo.

4. Come skipping down the stairs, pretty Peggy, oh,
Come skipping down the stairs, pretty Peggy, oh,
Come skipping down the stairs, combing back your yellow hair,
And bid farewell to Sweet William, oh.

5. Sweet William is dead, pretty Peggy, oh,
Sweet William is dead, pretty Peggy, oh,
Sweet William is dead, and he died for a maid,
The fairest maid in the areo.

6. If ever I return, pretty Peggy, oh,
If ever I return, pretty Peggy, oh,
If ever I return, all your cities I will burn
Destroying all the ladies in the areo.

John Riley

The returning soldier or sailor who disguises himself in order to test his sweetheart's fidelity has long been a favorite theme with ballad singers. Of course, everything turns out happily when she proves true and he reveals his real identity to her. To prove his identity, the 'long lost lover' usually shows her one half of a token which they broke between them at his departure.

KEY: C MINOR   CAPO: 3RD   PLAY: A MINOR   (LAWS N 42)

90

This then, sir, _____ was her re - ply. _____

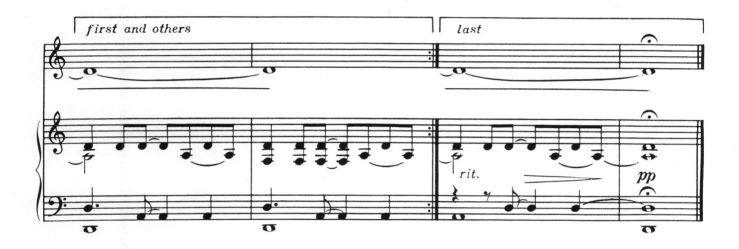

2. "Oh, no, kind sir, I cannot marry thee,
   For I've a love who sails all on the seas,
   He's been gone for seven years,
   Still no man shall marry me."

3. "What if he's in some battle slain,
   Or drownded in the deep salt sea?
   What if he's found another love,
   And he and his love both married be?"

4. "If he's in some battle slain,
   I will die when the moon doth wane.
   If he's drownded in the deep salt sea,
   I'll be true to his memory."

5. "And if he's found another love,
   And he and his love both married be,
   I wish them health and happiness
   Where they dwell across the sea."

6. He picked her up all in his arms,
   And kisses gave her, one, two, three,
   Saying, "Weep no more, my own true love,
   I am your long lost John Riley."

Willie Moore

Tragedy resulting from parental opposition to the marriage of two lovers was a favorite broadside theme. Though the text has the sound of British broadside balladry, the ballad of "Willie Moore" has been reported only in America, and rather rarely at that. One Ozark singer reported having met a Reverend William Moore who claimed the song was written about him. Such claims can usually be taken with a grain of salt.

KEY: F#   CAPO: 2ND   PLAY: E

Wil-lie Moore was a King

aged twen-ty one, Court-ed a maid-en fair,_____ Her

eyes were like two_ dia-monds bright, Ra-ven_black was her

*As performed: F(E) throughout song as a drone with the five-tone melody in the bass.

92

hair, hmm,hmm,hmm.

2. He courted her both day and night,
   To marry him she did agree,
   But when they went to get her parents' consent,
   They said, "This could never be," hmmm, hmmm, hmmm--.

3. "I love Willie Moore," sweet Annie replied,
   "Better than I love my life,
   And I would rather die than weep here and cry,
   Never to be his wife," hmmm, hmmm, hmmm--.

4. That very same night sweet Anne disappeared,
   They searched the country 'round
   In a little stream by the cabin door,
   The body of sweet Annie was found, hmmm, hmmm, hmmm--.

5. Sweet Annie's parents they live all alone,
   One mourns, the other cries,
   In a little green mound in front of their door
   The body of sweet Annie now lies.

6. Willie Moore scarce spoke that anyone knew,
   Soon from his friends did part,
   And the last heard of him was he's in Montreal,
   Where he died of a broken heart,
   hmmm, hmmm, hmmm--.

7. 7. Willie Moore was a king, etc.

Railroad Boy

Usually the villain of this piece is a 'butcher boy,' and the scene takes place in 'Jersey City.' Despite its localization in America, this ballad traces back to an amalgamation of two British broadsides: "The Squire's Daughter" and "There Is a Tavern in the Town."

KEY: D MINOR   CAPO: 5TH   PLAY: A MINOR   (LAWS P 24)

2. "Oh, mother dear, I cannot tell,
    It's that railroad boy that I love so well,
    He's courted me my life away
    And now at home he will not stay."

3. "There is a place in London town,
    Where that railroad boy goes
      and sits him down,
    He takes a strange girl on his knee,
    And he tells to her what he won't tell me."

4. Her father, he came home from work,
    Saying, "Where's my daughter,
      she seemed so hurt."
    He went upstairs to give her hope,
    And he found her hanging by a rope.

5. He took a knife and he cut her down
    And on her bosom these words he found:

6. "Go dig my grave both wide and deep,
    Put a marble stone at my head and feet,
    And at my breast put a white snow dove,
    To tell the world that I died of love."

*As performed: G(C).

Here is another familiar newspaper headline theme: "Jealous Lover Stabs Rival to Death." The broadside of yesteryear was the direct ancestor of today's newspapers, and headline stories have changed little since their earlier publication on English and Irish broadsides. This is a particularly handsome Ohio version of a ballad that should be better known.

The Lily of the West

KEY: Bb MINOR   CAPO: 6TH   PLAY: E MINOR   (LAWS P 29)

*Here, and throughout, the free piano transcription will differ considerably from performance with guitar.

mind. Her ro - sy cheeks, her ru - by lips, Like ar - rows pierced my breast___ And the name she bore was Flo - ra,___ The Lil - y of the West.___ 2. I

first and others | last

2. I courted lovely Flora some pleasure there to find,
But she turned unto another man which sore distressed my mind.
She robbed me of my liberty, deprived me of my rest—
Then go, my lovely Flora, the lily of the West.

3. 'Way down in yonder shady grove, a man of ~~high~~ *low* degree
Conversin' with my Flora there, it seemed so strange to me.
And the answer that she gave to him it sore did me oppress—
I was betrayed by Flora, the lily of the West.

4. I stepped up to my rival, my dagger in my hand,
I seized him by the collar, and boldly bade him stand.
Being mad to desperation I pierced him in the breast—
Then go, my lovely Flora, the lily of the West.

5. I had to stand my trial, I had to make my plea,
They placed me in the criminal box and then commenced on me.
Although she swore my life away, deprived me of my rest—
Still I love my faithless Flora, the lily of the West.

AMERICAN BALLADS AND SONGS

Native American folksongs and ballads result from a combination of several cultural strains meeting and coalescing under the unique conditions of American life and mores. The product is no less American when every now and then one catches a glimpse of the various strains which contributed to its being. Cowboy songs, bad men ballads, love lyrics, moonshining songs, Negro ballads, and hunting songs may be the product of a specific region, occupation, or status group, but cutting across all these levels there is something distinctly, perhaps peculiarly, recognizable in all of them which speaks for the land as a whole.

This is an American murdered girl ballad which omits the usual pregnant sweetheart theme. Here the young man kills the girl because she rejected his proposal, with other versions indicating family opposition to the marriage as the cause for her refusal to marry. Though similar in theme to various British broadside ballads, versions of this song have been reported only in America.

Banks of the Ohio

KEY: B   CAPO: 2ND   PLAY: A

Moderately

D(A)   A⁷(E)

I asked my love _____ to take a walk, _____

D(A)

_ to take a walk, _____ just a lit - tle walk, _____

D⁷(A⁷)   G (D)

_ Down be - side _____ where the wat - ers flow,

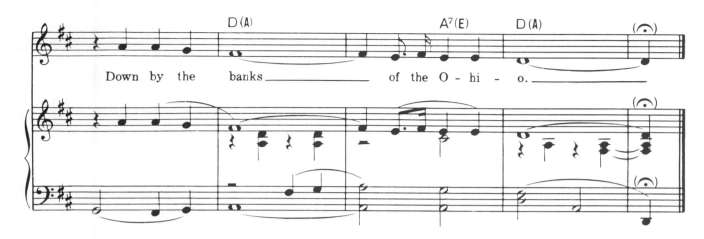

Down by the banks ———— of the O - hi - o. ————

Chorus:

And only say that you'll be mine
In no other's arms entwine,
Down beside where the waters flow,
Down by the banks of the Ohio.

2. I held a knife against her breast
As into my arms she pressed,
She cried, "Oh, Willie, don't murder me,
I'm not prepared for eternity."

And only say, etc.

3. I started home 'tween twelve and one,
I cried, "My God! what have I done?
Killed the only woman I loved,
Because she would not be my bride."

And only say, etc.

This is an American version of part of a British lyric song; additional verses to the original song can be found in "The Wagoner's Lad." In its present form, the song has been collected from New England farmers, southern mountaineers, western pioneers and cowboys. Some of its verses appear as folk lyrics in other songs.

Rambler Gambler

KEY: B   CAPO: 2ND   PLAY: A

I'm a ramb-ler,_____ I'm a gamb-ler,_____ I'm a long way____ from home,_____ And if peo-ple_____ don't like me_____ They can leave

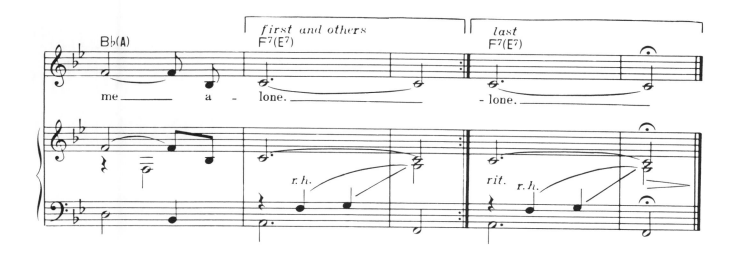

2. It's a dark night and it's lonesome,
   The moon gives no light,
   My pony won't travel
   This dark road tonight.

3. Well, I had me a little sweetheart,
   Her age was nineteen,
   She was the flower of Belton,
   The rose of Saleen.

4. But her parents didn't like me,
   Now she is the same,
   If I'm writ in your book, love,
   Just you blot out my name.

5. I'm a rambler, I'm a gambler, etc.

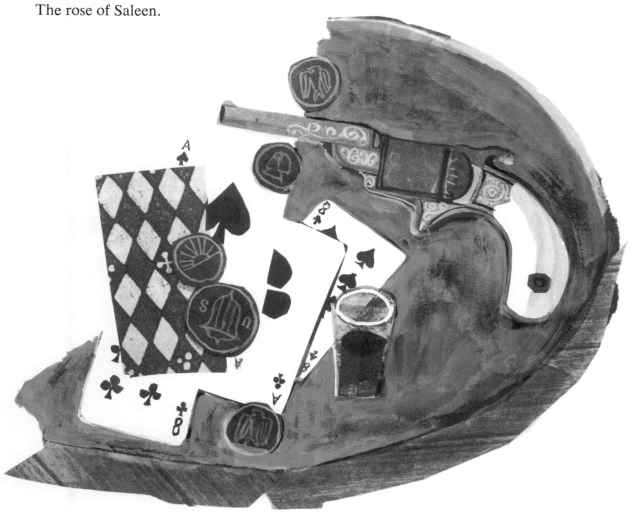

Alan Lomax collected a version of this song from a miner's daughter in Kentucky in 1937. Subsequently it was adapted to a form which was popularized by Josh White. The song has made its round across the nation for more than twenty years among city singers of folk songs, but its possible origins remain an enigma.

KEY: D MINOR   CAPO: NONE (6TH STRING TUNED D)   PLAY: D MINOR

*As performed: A⁷ against sung Am, common in blues.

2.   If I had listened to what my mother said,
    I'd have been at home today,
    But I was young and foolish, oh God,
    Let a rambler lead me astray.

3.   Go tell my baby sister,
    Don't do what I have done,
    But shun that house in New Orleans,
    They call the Rising Sun.

4.   I'm goin' back to New Orleans,
    My race is almost run,
    I'm goin' back to spend my life
    Beneath that Rising Sun.

This is Woody Guthrie's version of a cowboy song about which very little is known. One of Vance Randolph's Ozark singers told him it was already "an old song in 1893." The story of the pioneer woman who fought beside her menfolk is as much real history as romance. In other versions the woman is killed by Indians, after which the cowboys ride out to avenge her death.

Ranger's Command

KEY: F#   CAPO: 4TH   PLAY: D

2.   To hold a six-shooter and never to run
       As long as there's bullets in both of your guns.

      3.   I met a fair maiden whose name I don't know,
            I asked her to the round-up with me would she go,

4.   She said she'd go with me to the cold round-up,
       And drink that hard liquor from a cold bitter cup.

      5.   We started for the round-up in the Fall of the year,
            Expecting to get there with a herd of fat steer,

6.   When the rustlers broke on us in the dead hour of night
       She rose from her warm bed a battle to fight.

      7.   She rose from her warm bed
               with a gun in each hand,
          Saying, "Come all of you cowboys,
               and fight for your land."

8.   Come all of you cowboys, and don't ever run,
       As long as there's bullets in both of your guns.

Here's a modern ballad that sounds a lot like a television drama or a movie plot, but in true ballad style it capsules all the details in a few stanzas. The accused, but innocent, man can't supply an alibi for his whereabouts at the time of a murder simply because he was in the arms of his best friend's wife. Is he to be pitied for his naïveté or to be admired for his gallantry? The ballad is the work of Marijon Wilkins and Danny Dill.

Long Black Veil

KEY: D   CAPO: NONE   PLAY: D

Refrain *(for 4th and 6th verses)*

*As performed: Ab(G).
**As performed: Eb(D) throughout.

no - bod - y sees, ____ No - bod-y knows but

me. _____

into 5th verse

D.S. last

5. The _

D.S.

3.   The judge said, "Son, what is your alibi?
     If you were somewheres else, then you won't have to die."

4.   I spoke not a word, though it meant my life,
     For I'd been in the arms of my best friend's wife.

     She walks these hills in a long black veil,
     Visits my grave when the night winds wail,
     Nobody knows, nobody sees,
     Nobody knows, but me.

5.   The scaffold is high, eternity near,
     She stands in the crowd, she sheds not a tear,

6.   But sometimes at night,
        when the cold winds moan,
     In a long black veil she cries o'er my bones.

     She walks these hills, etc.

Railroad Bill

The original "Railroad Bill" is said to have been a Negro turpentine worker from Alabama at the end of the 19th century. His career of crime had its Robin Hood overtones, but he killed one too many sheriffs and they finally cut him down. To the southern Negro he became a symbol of a black man who had bucked white authority and who had been too smart to get caught. His ballad travelled out of Alabama into the southern mountains where its narrative details fell by the way until it became a popular instrumental show piece with just a few disconnected verses held over from the original ballad.

KEY: E♭   CAPO: 3RD   PLAY: C

*As performed: E♭(C) to end.

2. Railroad Bill, Railroad Bill,
   He never work' and he never will,
   Ride, ride, ride.

3. Kill me a chicken, send me the wing,
   You think I'm workin', I don't do a thing,
   Ride, ride, ride.

4. Railroad Bill, Railroad Bill,
   Live way up on Railroad Hill,
   Ride, ride, ride.

Charles "Pretty Boy" Floyd of Sallisaw, Oklahoma, was a convicted criminal at the age of twenty. His crimes included bank robbery and murder, but the folk made a hero of him. In composing this ballad, Woody Guthrie portrayed Floyd as many Oklahomans saw him—a modern day Robin Hood. The ballad contains one of Woody's most memorable lines: "Some rob you with a six-gun, some with a fountain pen."

Pretty Boy Floyd

KEY: F   CAPO: 5TH   PLAY: C

*As performed: D⁷(G⁷).

Come gath-er round _____ me,
chil - dren, _____ a sto-ry I will tell, _____ of Pret-ty Boy Floyd, an out-law, _____ Ok-la -

*As performed: $D^7(G^7)$.

ho-ma knew him well.

2. Was in the town of Shawnee,
On a Saturday afternoon,
His wife beside him in the wagon,
As into town they rode.

3. A deputy sheriff approached them,
In a manner rather rude,
Using vulgar words of language,
And his wife she overheard.

4. Well, Pretty Boy grabbed a long chain,
And the deputy grabbed a gun,
And in the fight that followed,
He laid that deputy down.

5. Then he took to the trees and rivers,
To live a life of shame,
Every crime in Oklahoma,
Was added to his name.

6. Yes, he took to the trees and timbers
On the Canadian river shore,
And the outlaw found a welcome
At many a farmer's door.

7. Yes, there's many a starving farmer,
The same story told,
How the outlaw paid their mortgage,
And saved their little home.

8. Others tell about the stranger,
Who came to beg a meal,
And underneath his napkin
Left a thousand-dollar bill.

9. It was in Oklahoma City,
It was on a Christmas day,
Came a whole carload of groceries,
And a letter that did say:

10. "Well, you say that I'm an outlaw,
And you say that I'm a thief,
Here's a Christmas dinner,
For the families on relief."

11. Well, as through this world I've rambled,
I've seen lots of funny men,
Some rob you with a six-gun,
Some with a fountain pen.

12. As through this world you travel,
As through this world you roam,
You'll never see an outlaw
Drive a family from their home.

Here, in song, are a moonshiner's recipe and instructions for making whiskey. It was written by Albert Frank Beddoe and included by him in a little known collection of ballads from Bexar County, Texas. Its present popularity places it first on the moonshiner's hit parade.

Copper Kettle

KEY: D   CAPO: NONE   PLAY D

(A*) not actually played, but indicated by bass run of guitar.

ju-ni-per _____ while the moon is bright,

Watch them jugs a - fill-in' _____ in the pale moon-light.

**As performed: Gm(F♯m).

2. My Daddy he made whiskey,
    My Granddaddy did too,
    We ain't paid no whiskey tax
    Since seventeen ninety-two.

    We just lay there by the juniper, etc.

3. Build you a fire with hickory,
    Hickory and ash and oak,
    Don't use no green or rotten wood,
    They'll get you by the smoke

    While you lay there by the juniper, etc.

4. Get you a copper kettle,
    Get you a copper coil,
    Cover with new-made corn mash,
    And never more you'll toil.

    You'll just lay there by the juniper, etc.

Wildwood Flower

Though known widely throughout the southern mountains, little is known about the origin of this charming piece. Folklorists think it may have circulated as sheet music or in some parlor song books, but their thesis is unsupported by any known printed versions until the 1930s. The degree of variation in known texts and some curious verbal corruptions suggest it has existed in oral tradition for some time, whatever its ultimate source may have been.

KEY: B   CAPO: 4TH   PLAY: G

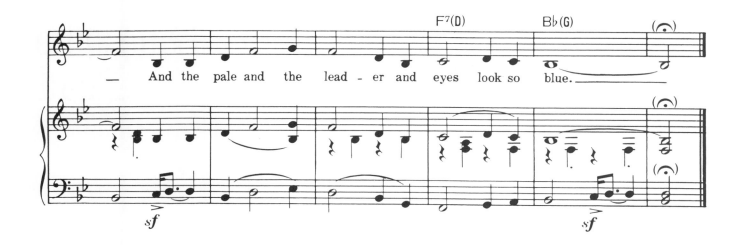

And the pale and the lead-er and eyes look so blue.

2. I will dance, I will sing and my life shall be gay,
   I will charm every heart, in its crown I will sway,
   I woke from my dream and all idols was clay,
   And all portions of lovin' had all flown away.

3. He taught me to love him and promised to love
   And cherish me over all other above,
   My poor heart is wondering, no misery can tell,
   He left me no warning, no words of farewell.

4. He taught me to love him and called me his flower,
   That was blooming to cheer him through life's
        weary hour,
   How I long to see him and regret the dark hour,
   He's gone and neglected his frail wildwood flower.

This lover's lament traces back to a Negro "Jubilee" song, a short-line spiritual from the immediate post Civil War period. In the course of its secularization, the song has become extremely popular among white singers in the South and Midwest, as well as remaining a staple with Negro singers in the deep South.

Lonesome Road

KEY: E   CAPO: 4TH   PLAY: C

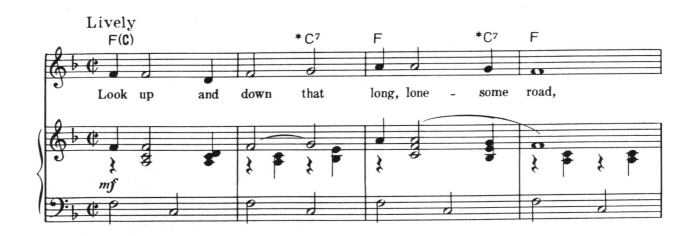

Look up and down that long, lone - some road,

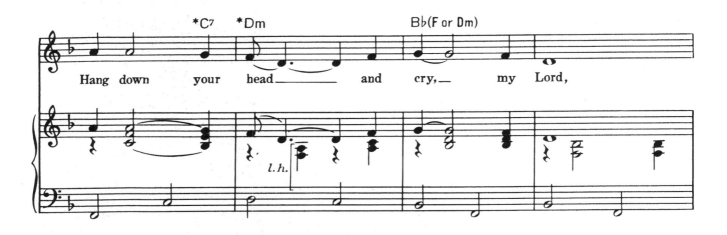

Hang down your head_____ and cry,___ my Lord,

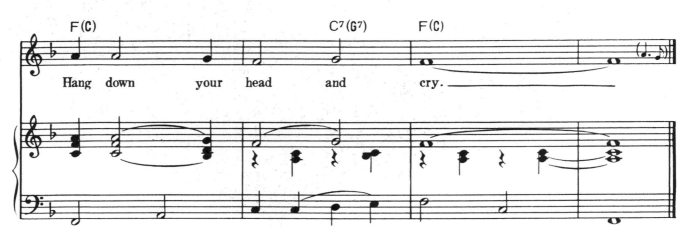

Hang down your head and cry._____

*As performed: F(C) throughout.

2.	They say all good friends must part some time,
Why not you and I, my lord,
Why not you and I?

3.	Oh, I wish to the lord that I'd never been born,
Or died when I was a baby, my lord,
Or died when I was a baby.

4.	I would not be here eatin' this cold cornbread
Or soppin' this salty gravy, my lord,
Or soppin' this salty gravy.

5.	Oh, I wish to the lord that I'd never seen your face,
Or heard your lyin' tongue, my lord,
Heard your lyin' tongue.

6.	You'd better look up and down that long lonesome road,
Where all of your friends have gone, my lord,
And you and I must go.

7.	You'd better look up and down that long lonesome road,
Hang down your head and cry, my lord,
Hang down your head and cry.

Hill people and back country folk used to live off hunting, and a good hound dog was worth his weight in gold in helping them to track and catch food. No wonder they wrote paeans of praise in his honor, and mourned his death in song. "Old Blue" is known throughout the rural South, from Alabama to Texas, by white and Negro folk alike.

Old Blue

KEY: D   CAPO: NONE   PLAY: D

2. Shouldered my gun and I tooted my horn,
   Gonna find a 'possum in the new-ground corn,
   Old Blue barked and I went to see,
   Cornered a 'possum up in a tree.

   Come on Blue, you good dog, you.

3. Old Blue died, and he died so hard,
   Shook the ground in my back yard,
   Dug his grave with a silver spade,
   Lowered him down with links of chain.

   Every link, I did call his name,
   Here Blue, you good dog, you,
   Here Blue, I'm a-comin' there too.

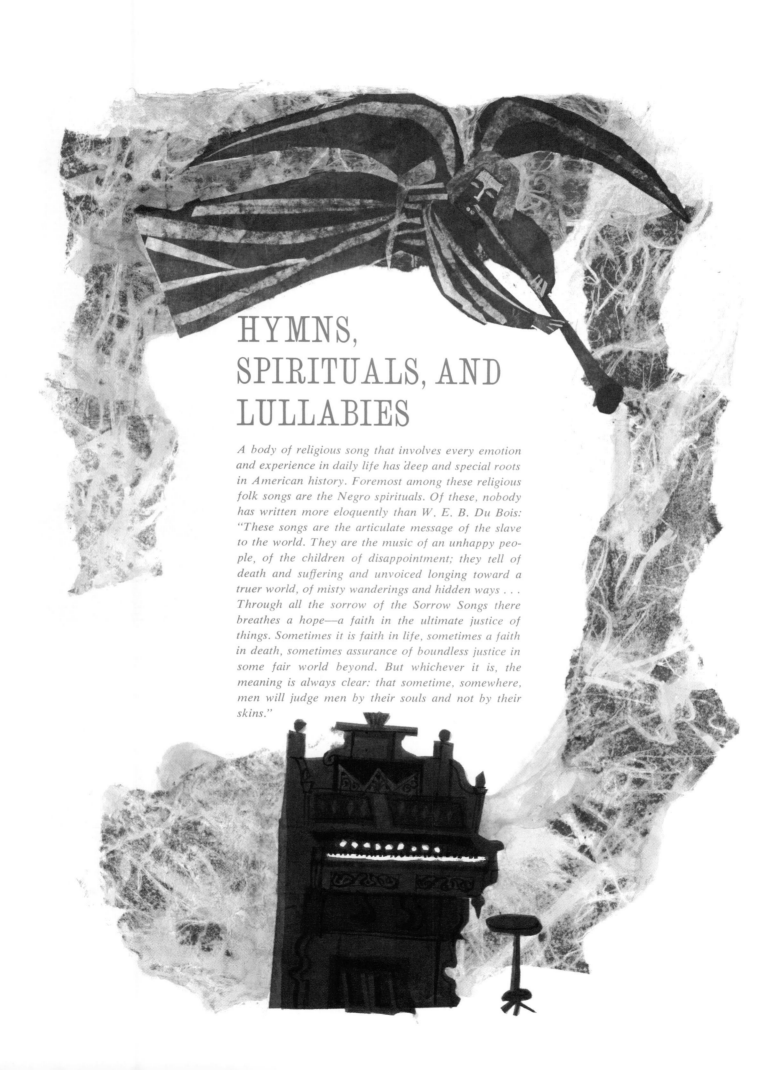

HYMNS, SPIRITUALS, AND LULLABIES

A body of religious song that involves every emotion and experience in daily life has deep and special roots in American history. Foremost among these religious folk songs are the Negro spirituals. Of these, nobody has written more eloquently than W. E. B. Du Bois: "These songs are the articulate message of the slave to the world. They are the music of an unhappy people, of the children of disappointment; they tell of death and suffering and unvoiced longing toward a truer world, of misty wanderings and hidden ways . . . Through all the sorrow of the Sorrow Songs there breathes a hope—a faith in the ultimate justice of things. Sometimes it is faith in life, sometimes a faith in death, sometimes assurance of boundless justice in some fair world beyond. But whichever it is, the meaning is always clear: that sometime, somewhere, men will judge men by their souls and not by their skins."

This spiritual-lullaby probably originated in the ante-bellum South, from where it was transported to the West Indies. It appears to have died out in this country only to be discovered in the Bahamas. From there it was reintroduced to us, eventually becoming one of the standards of the popular folk song movement.

All My Trials

KEY: C#   CAPO: 1ST   PLAY: C

Flowing, with a moderate calypso beat

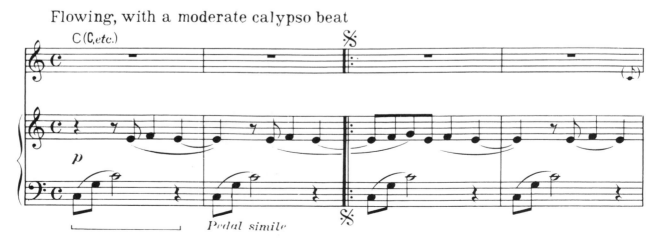

(after 3rd and 5th verses only)

Too late, my broth-ers,

Too late but nev-er mind,

All my tri-als, Lord,

Soon be

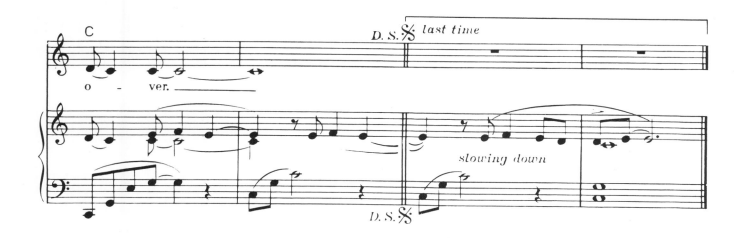

2. The river of Jordan is muddy and cold,
   Well, it chills the body, but not the soul,
   All my trials, Lord, soon be over.

3. I've got a little book with pages three,
   And every page spells liberty,
   All my trials, Lord, soon be over.

   Too late my brothers,
   Too late, but never mind
   All my trials, Lord, soon be over.

4. If living were a thing that money
         could buy,
   You know the rich would live
         and the poor would die,
   All my trials, Lord, soon be over.

5. There grows a tree in Paradise,
   And the Pilgrims call it the tree of life,
   All my trials, Lord, soon be over.

   Too late, my brothers, etc.

Kumbaya

As in the case of "All My Trials," this song had to travel to foreign lands and be brought back to us before it achieved its rightful place in our songlore. It started as a Negro gospel song, "Come By Here, Lord," was exported to the West Indies where it was rephrased in 'pidgin-English' as "Kumbaya," and returned to the United States where it is now a great favorite with city singers.

KEY: D   CAPO: NONE   PLAY: D

*As performed: Bb, Eb, Bb,(A, D, A).

Someone's singing Lord, Kumbaya (3)
Oh, Lord, Kumbaya

Kumbaya, my Lord, Kumbaya (3)
Oh, Lord, Kumbaya

Someone's praying Lord, Kumbaya (3)
Oh, Lord, Kumbaya

Kumbaya, my Lord, Kumbaya (3)
Oh, Lord, Kumbaya

Someone's sleeping Lord, Kumbaya (3)
Oh, Lord, Kumbaya

Kumbaya, my Lord, Kumbaya (3)
Oh, Lord, Kumbaya

Numerous composers, great and small, have tried their hand at preparing a musical setting for "The Lord's Prayer," with varying degrees of success. Perhaps the best known setting is that of Alfred Hay Malotte. But for sheer excitement none approaches this West-Indian style setting by an anonymous composer.

Hallowed Be Thy Name

KEY: F#   CAPO: 1ST   PLAY: E

Thy King - dom come, Thy will be __ done, ____

D.C.

2. On Earth as it is in Heaven, (Hallowèd . . .)
   Give us this day our daily bread, (Hallowèd . . .)

3. And forgive us all our trespasses (Hallowèd . . .)
   As we forgive those who trespass against us, (Hallowèd . . .)

4. And lead us not unto the devil to be tempted, (Hallowèd . . .)
   But deliver us from all that is evil. (Hallowèd . . .)

5. For Thine is the Kingdom, the Power and the Glory (Hallowèd . . .)
   Forever, forever, forever and ever. (Hallowèd . . .)

6. Amen, Amen, Amen, Amen, (Hallowèd . . .)
   Amen, Amen, Amen, Amen,
   Hallowèd be Thy name.

This song has long been one of the favorites of Negro street singers and itinerant preachers throughout the United States. It was recorded by blind street minstrels in the early days of 'race' records, and these recordings undoubtedly affected the oral circulation of the song. The reference is to the City of Heaven mentioned in the New Testament, for which see Revelations 21 : 13, 14.

KEY: F   CAPO: 1ST   PLAY: E

Twelve Gates to the City

Three gates in - to the East,

Three gates in - to the West,

Three gates in - to the North,   Three gates in - to the

Well, oh what a beautiful City, etc.

2. See those children yonder,
    They all dressed in red,
    They must be the children,
    Children that Moses led,
    You know, there're Twelve Gates into the City, Allelu---.

    Well, oh what a beautiful City, etc.

3. When I get to Heaven,
    I'm going to sing and shout,
    There ain't nobody up there
    Who's going to put me out.
    You know, there're Twelve Gates to the City, Allelu---.

    Well, oh what a beautiful City, etc.

Peggy Seeger helped to make this Christmas spiritual popular, borrowing it from "American Folk Songs for Christmas" compiled by her mother,
Ruth Crawford Seeger. The song dates from the end of the 19th century,
and is a fine example of the folk Negro's attitude toward his religion—
a religion in which he is on personal terms with his Saviour, speaking
familiarly to Him and about Him, much as if He were a man down the
street.

Virgin Mary

KEY: A MINOR   CAPO: NONE   PLAY: A MINOR

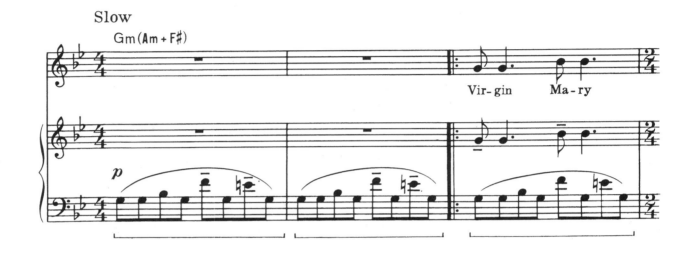

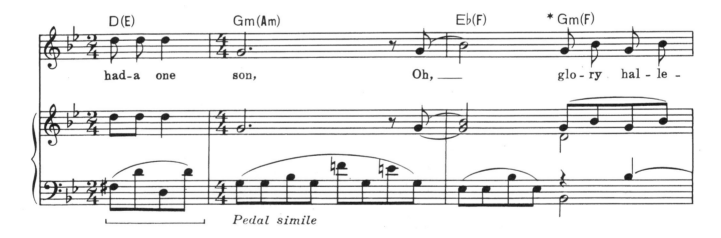

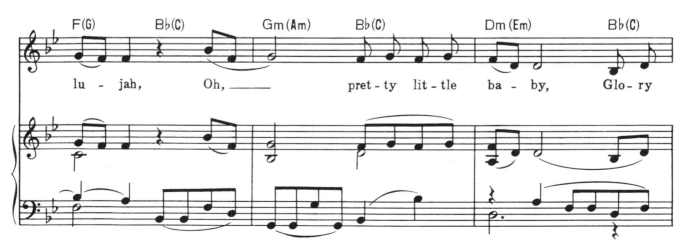

*As performed: Eb(F).

2. "Well, Mary how you call that pretty little baby,
   Oh -, pretty little baby,
   Oh -, pretty little baby,
   Glory be to the new-born King."

3. "Well, some call Him Jesus, think I'll call Him Savior
   Oh -, I think I'll call Him Savior
   Oh -, I think I'll call Him Savior,
   Glory be to the new-born King."

4. Riding from the East there came three wise men,
   Oh -, came three wise men,
   Oh -, came three wise men,
   Glory be to the new-born King.

5. Said, "Follow that star, you'll surely find the baby,
   Oh -, surely find the baby,
   Oh -, surely find the baby,
   Glory be to the new-born King."

6. Well, the Virgin Mary had-a one son, etc.

The Negro spiritual, like the Anglo-American lyric folksong, is frequently a patchwork of commonplace phrases and lines. This song is a perfect example of such patchwork, for it contains lines and stanzas (e.g., 'Jordan River,' 'Jacob's Ladder,' 'Golden Crown,' etc.) usually found either by themselves or in combination with still other commonplace spiritual expressions. In this manner the Negro religious singer could slowly bring songs into being, adding bit by bit to standard phrases until the accretions created something entirely new.

We Are Crossing Jordan River

KEY: E♭   CAPO: 1ST   PLAY: D

2. Now when I get to Heaven
    I'm gonna sit down on that golden throne $\}$(2)
    Jordan River, chilly and cold,
    Chills the body but not the soul.
    We are crossing, etc.

3. We are climbing Jacob's ladder,
    I want to sit down on that golden throne $\}$(2)
    Jordan River, deep and wide,
    I got a home on the other side.
    We are crossing, etc.

4. We are crossing etc.

Versions of this song were recorded by street singers in the '20s and '30s, from which recordings the song has become popular in the present folk song movement. The metaphor of the 'storm' appears rather frequently in Negro religious song. The term should not be taken literally, for it refers to 'the storm of life.' Other spirituals utilizing this phrase make it clear that the only way out of the 'storm' is through belief in and observance of the Lord's word.

Somebody Got Lost in a Storm

KEY: C#   CAPO: FIRST   PLAY: C

*As performed: A⁷(G⁷).

2.　Poor sinner got lost in a storm, etc.

4.　Don't ever get lost in a storm, etc.

3.　Somebody got lost in a storm, etc.

5.　Somebody got lost in a storm, etc.

Numerous songs have been borrowed from the church and with a few verbal changes have been put to use as Wobbly songs, union songs, picket-line songs, and most recently as integration songs. This is one of the best of such songs, which saw service earlier in union halls and is now widely sung by whites and Negroes in the civil rights movement. Zilphia Horton first heard it at the Highlander Folk School in Tennessee in 1947 from members of the Food and Tobacco Workers Union, who based it on one of the stanzas of a hymn which began "We will overcome." From then on numerous verses have been 'zipped in' as needed.

We Shall Overcome

KEY: B   CAPO: 2ND   PLAY: A

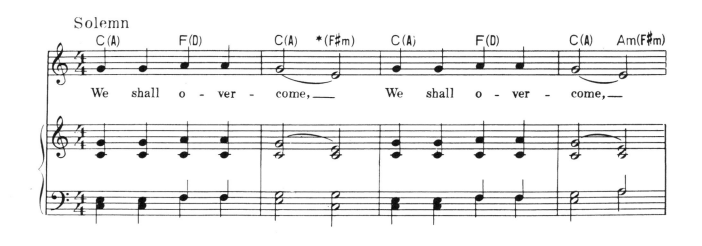

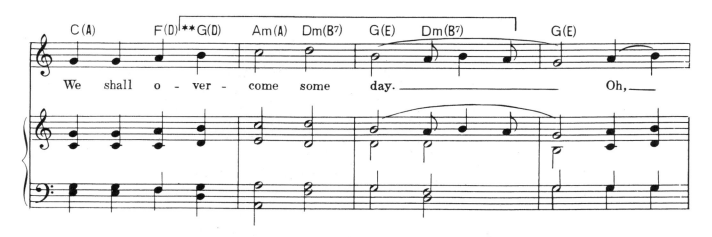

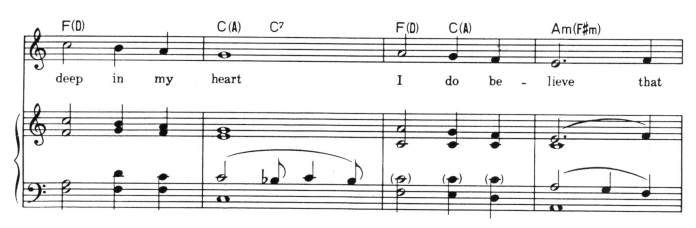

*As performed: Am(F#m).
**As performed: F,C,D,G,D(D,A,B7),E,B7).

2. We'll walk hand in hand, we'll walk hand in hand,
    We'll walk hand in hand, some day.
    Oh, deep in my heart I do believe,
    That we shall overcome some day.

3. We are not afraid, we are not afraid,
    We are not afraid, today.
    Oh, deep in my heart I do believe
    That we shall overcome some day.

4. We shall overcome, etc.

(*Additional verses*)

We shall live in peace . . .

The truth will make us free . . .

We shall brothers be . . .

This charming cradle song has been collected mainly in the South but has become what may be the best known lullaby in America. Cecil Sharp collected it in Virginia and North Carolina in the fall of 1918, and the song has since been recorded from Alabama to Texas. Most recently it has been found as the text of ball-bouncing and skip-rope games, and a Rock and Roll version has even been recorded commercially.

KEY: C   CAPO: NONE   PLAY: C

Hush Little Baby

2.   If that diamond ring is brass,
       Papa's going to buy you a looking-glass.
       If that looking-glass gets broke,
       Papa's going to buy you a billy-goat.

3.   If that billy-goat don't pull,
       Papa's going to buy you a cart and bull.
       If that cart and bull turn over,
       Papa's going to buy you a dog named Rover.

4.   If that dog named Rover don't bark,
       Papa's going to buy you a horse and cart,
       If that horse and cart fall down,
       You'll still be the sweetest little baby in town.

Julia Ward Howe was sitting in her hotel room in Washington listening to soldiers singing "John Brown's Body" as they marched to the front in December of 1861. As she watched and listened, a poem shaped itself in her mind and she rapidly put it down on a scrap of paper. It was later published in the Atlantic Monthly, and has since become one of America's most stirring songs.

Battle Hymn of the Republic

KEY: F#   CAPO: 2ND   PLAY: E

With majesty

Mine eyes have seen the glo - ry of the com - ing of the Lord, He is tram - pling out the vin - tage where the grapes of wrath are stored, He has loosed the fate - ful light - ning of His

*As performed: Gm(C#m).
**As performed: Eb(A).

2.   In the beauty of the lilies Christ was born across the sea,
    With a glory in His bosom that transfigures you and me.
    As He died to make man holy let us die to make men free,
    His truth is marching on.
    Glory, glory, etc.

The text of this white Protestant hymn was written by John Newton (1725-1807) and has frequently been published in shape note and other hymnals since the early years of the 19th century. The tune is anonymous but is related to several Scottish secular melodies tracing from the 18th century. When sung in Negro churches across the country, it is usually performed to a tune which is closely related to the white melody but is sung more slowly and embellished in "Old Hundred" style. This version was collected by John Cohen in Kentucky. Joan Baez sings it without accompaniment.

Amazing Grace

A - maz - ing grace, _____ how sweet the sound _____ To

save a wretch like me, _____ To save a _____ wretch _____ like _____ me. _

_ I once was lost but now I'm found, _____ I

once was_ lost _____ but _____ now_ I'm _ found, Was

(similar dynamics throughout ad lib.)

blind but now I see, _____ Was blind _____ but now I _____

see. That pre - cious day that grace ap - peared, _____ That

pre - cious day _____ that _____ grace ap - peared, The

hour I first be - lieved, _____ The hour _____ I _____ first _ be -

lieved, 'Twas grace that taught my heart to fear, ___ 'Twas grace that

taught ___ my_ heart to __ fear, And grace my fears re -

lieved, ___ And grace ___ my_ fears re - lieved.

Through ma - ny dan - gers, toils and snares, ___ Through __

ma - ny dan - gers,_ toils and_ snares, I have al - rea - dy

come, __ I have al - rea - dy _____ come._

_ 'Tis grace that's brought me safe this far, __ 'Tis grace that's

brought ___ me safe this far, And grace will lead me

home, __ And grace _____ will lead _ me_ home.

MODERN AND COMPOSED SONGS

For almost a century, the folklorists have debated the origins of folk song, with some believing that folk music is created collectively and others taking up the cudgels for individual authorship. Both are right, of course, for folk music is created both individually and communally. Here are some striking examples of modern and/or composed songs which have been accepted and welcomed by the community, and which are perhaps in process of becoming folk songs.

In a few short verses we have the story of a life—birth, marriage, children, war and death. This vignette is the work of Jack Elliott's old side-kick, Derroll Adams, folk singer and song writer from Portland, Oregon, who today makes his home in Belgium.

Portland Town

KEY: F MINOR   CAPO: 1ST   PLAY: E MINOR

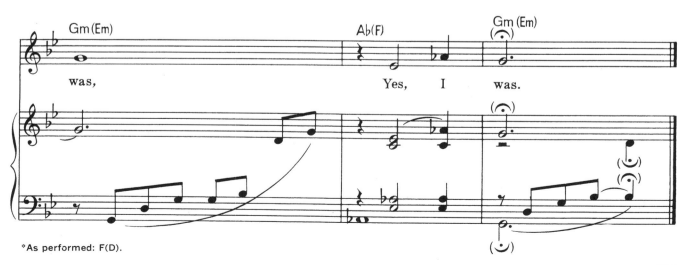

*As performed: F(D).

2.   I was born in Portland town,
          Got married in Portland town,
          Yes I did, yes I did,
          Yes, I did.

3.   Got married in Portland town,
          Had children one, two, three,
          Yes I did, yes I did,
          Yes, I did.

4.   They sent them away to war,
          Ain't got no kids no more,
          No I ain't, no I ain't,
          No, I ain't.

5.   I was born in Portland town,
          I was born in Portland town,
          Yes I was, yes I was,
          Yes, I was.

This song is typical of the exciting 'Highlife' music heard in the cafes of Ghana. It shows the influence of American jazz and Latin American rhythms on West African native musics, indicating a direction in musical diffusion which ethnomusicologists are first beginning to notice after years of studying the movement in the reverse direction, from Africa to America. Its poetry, too, is worthy of notice for it exhibits a fluidity of words and metaphors based on ordinary speech patterns which strike home directly, if sometimes savagely.

Danger Waters

KEY: E♭   CAPO: 1ST   PLAY: D

And I holler, "Why?" etc.

2. First we go in a room,
    Make me Momma no know,
    Make me lie on a sofa,
    Make me have-a me labor.

    And I holler, "Why?" etc.

3. Give me back me shillin',
    Give me back me shillin',
    You can stand on your own feet now,
    Give me back me shillin'.

    And I holler, "Why?" etc.

4. Hold me tight, hold me tight,
    Danger waters coming, baby, hold me tight,
    Hold me tight, hold me tight,
    Danger waters coming, baby, hold me.

    And I holler, "Why?" etc. (2)

Where Have All the Flowers Gone?

Pete Seeger got the idea for this song from a verse of an old song quoted by Mikhail Sholokhov in "And Quiet Flows the Don." The original words in translation are: "Where are the geese? They've gone to the reeds. And where are the reeds? They've been gathered by the girls. And where are the girls? They've taken husbands. And where are the Cossacks? They've gone to war." Similar circular-question songs are found in the works of folk and art composers and poets in many parts of the world.

KEY: B   CAPO: 2ND   PLAY: A

*As performed: Guitar retains F(D).

2. Where have all the young girls gone, long time passing,
    Where have all the young girls gone, long time ago,
    Where have all the young girls gone, gone to young men every one,
    When will they ever learn, when will they ever learn?

3. Where have all the young men gone, long time passing,
    Where have all the young men gone, long time ago,
    Where have all the young men gone, they are all in uniform,
    When will they ever learn, when will they ever learn?

4. Where have all the soldiers gone, long time passing
    Where have all the soldiers gone, long time ago,
    Where have all the soldiers gone, gone to graveyards every one
    When will they ever learn, when will they ever learn?

5. Where have all the graveyards gone, long time passing,
    Where have all the graveyards gone, long time ago,
    Where have all the graveyards gone, covered with flowers every one
    When will they ever learn, when will they ever learn?

6. Where have all the flowers gone, etc.

Early in the history of recorded hillbilly music, white mountain musicians and singers began to create their own religious songs based largely on biblical narrative. Their influence has continued to this day. One of the best of these modern gospel songs is this composition by Grady and Hazel Cole, based on the Dives and Lazarus story and the death of Christ. The last verse is a recent addition to the song.

The Tramp on the Street

KEY: C#   CAPO: 1ST   PLAY: C

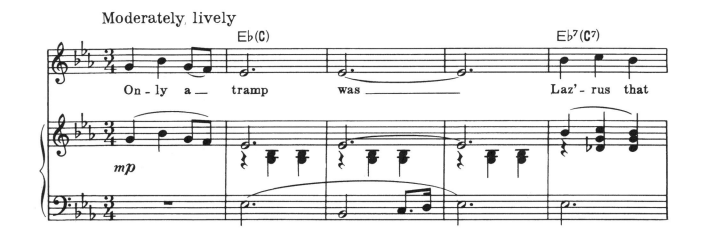

(F#*) and (G*) played by sliding in barre position from (F).

He was somebody's darlin', he was some mother's son,
Once he was fair, and once he was young,
Some mother she rocked him, her little darlin' to sleep,
But they left him to die like a tramp in the street.

2.   Jesus who died on Calvary's Tree,
Shed His life-blood for you and for me,
They pierced His side, His hands and His feet
And they left Him to die like a tramp on the street.

He was Mary's own darlin', he was God's chosen Son,
Once He was fair and once He was young,
Mary she rocked Him, her little darlin' to sleep,
But they left Him to die like a tramp on the street.

3.   When the battles are over and the victory's won
Everyone mourns for the poor man's son,
Red, White and Blue and victory's sweet,
And they left him to die like a tramp on the street.

He was somebody's darlin', he was some mother's son, etc.

The hardships and heartbreaks of people who earn their living off the sea have never been as starkly and dramatically described as in this poem by the 19th century English clergyman and novelist, Charles Kingsley. The music was composed by the English musician, singer and music teacher, John Hullah.

Three Fishers

KEY: A   CAPO: 2ND   PLAY: G

Moderately

Three fish-ers went sail-ing out in-to the west, Out in-to the west as the sun went down, Each thought on the wom-an that loved him the best, And the

children stood watching them out of the town. For men must work and women must weep, For there's little to earn and many to keep, And the harbor bar be moaning. 2. Three

*As performed: B♭(G).
**As performed: E♭(C).

2.   Three wives sat up in the lighthouse tower,
    They trimmed the lamps as the sun went down,
    And they looked at the squall and they looked at the shower,
    And the night-wrack came rolling in ragged and brown.

    For men must work and women must weep,
    'Though storms be sudden and the waters be deep
    And the harbor bar be moaning.

3.   Three corpses lay out on the shining sand,
    In the morning gleam as the tide went down,
    And the women were weeping and wringing their hands,
    For those who would never come back to the town.

    For men must work and women must weep,
    And the sooner it's over, the sooner to sleep
    And good-bye to that bar and its moaning.

Donna Donna

This song, composed for the Yiddish musical theatre by Sholom Secunda, has long been a favorite with Jewish folk singers. Several translations have been attempted by various singers, but none tell the tale so well as this one by Arthur Kevess and Teddi Schwartz.

KEY: B MINOR   CAPO: 2ND   PLAY: A MINOR

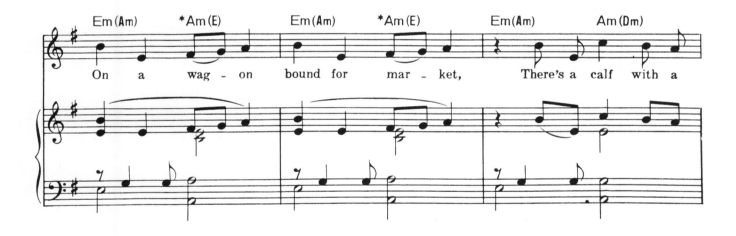

On a wag - on bound for mar - ket, There's a calf with a

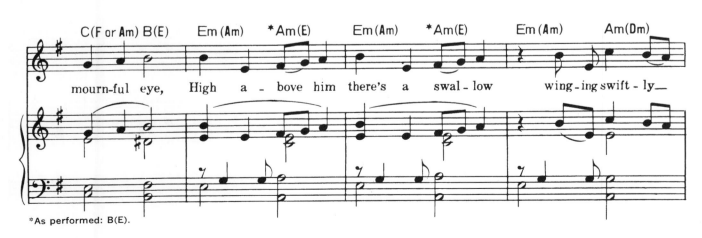

mourn-ful eye, High a - bove him there's a swal - low wing - ing swift - ly—

*As performed: B(E).

167

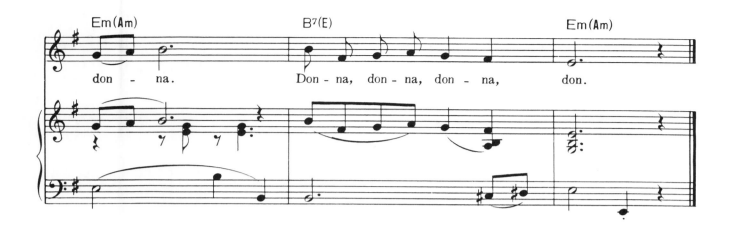

don - na.   Don - na, don - na, don - na,   don.

2.   "Stop complaining," said the farmer, "Who told you a calf to be,
     Why don't you have wings to fly with, like the swallow so proud and free?"
     How the winds are laughing, they laugh with all their might,
     Laugh and laugh the whole day through, and half the Summer's night.

     Donna, Donna, Donna, Donna; Donna, Donna, Donna, Don—— (2)

3.   Calves are easily bound and slaughtered, never knowing the reason why,
     But whoever treasures freedom, like the swallow has learned to fly,
     How the winds are laughing, they laugh with all their might,
     Laugh and laugh the whole day through, and half the Summer's night.

     Donna, etc.

A number of topical song writers have commented on the dangers of fall-out and the death and sickness which rides with radioactive winds and rain. Malvina Reynolds is one of the few to successfully capture the feeling of the potential tragedy by her simple story of a little boy and the grass around him which disappears in "the gentle rain that falls for years."

What Have They Done to the Rain?

KEY: B   CAPO: NONE; GUITAR TUNED DOWN ½ TONE   PLAY: C

Moderately

Bb(C)　　　　　　　　　　Cm(Dm)　　　*Dm(G)

Just a lit-tle rain fall-ing all a - round, ___ The

(Em)　　　　F(G)　　　Bb(C)

grass lifts its head ___ to the heav - en - ly sound,

Gm(Am)　　　　　　　Dm(Em)

Just a lit-tle rain, just a lit-tle rain,

Eb(F)　　　　　　F(G)

What have they done ___ to the rain? ___

*As performed: F(G).

what have they done to the rain? _____

2. Just a little breeze out of the sky,
The leaves nod their heads as the breeze blows by,
Just a little breeze with some smoke in its eye,
What have they done to the rain?

Just a little boy standing in the rain,
The gentle rain that falls for years, etc.

In a short life of only 40 years, Edgar Allan Poe secured a prominent place for himself as a literary critic, an idealistic and romantic poet, and one of the most powerful and compelling mystery and fantasy tale tellers. Of his poetic creations, perhaps only "The Raven" is better known than his tragic love poem, "Annabel Lee." The musical setting given here was composed by Don Dilworth.

Annabel Lee

KEY: G# MINOR   CAPO: NONE   PLAY: G# MINOR (BARRE)

*As performed: F(F#).

2. For I was a child and she was a child,
   In this kingdom by the sea:
   But we loved with a love that was more than love—
   I and my Annabel Lee:
   With a love that the winged seraphs of heaven
   Coveted her and me.

3. And this is the reason that, long ago,
   In this kingdom by the sea)
   A wind blew out of a cloud,
   Chilling my Annabel Lee:
   So that her high-born kinsmen came
   And bore her away from me,
   To shut her up in a sepulcher
   In this kingdom by the sea.

4. And the angels, not half so happy in heaven,
   Went envying her and me—
   Yes—that was the reason (as all men know,
   In this kingdom by the sea)
   That the wind came out of the cloud by night,
   Chilling my Annabel Lee
   That the wind came out of the cloud by night,
   Killing my Annabel Lee

5. But our love it was stronger by far than the love
   Of those who were older than we—
   Of many far wiser than we—
   Of many far wiser than we.
   And neither the angels in heaven above,
   Nor the demons down under the sea,
   Can ever dissever my soul from the soul
   Of the beautiful Annabel Lee

6. And the moon never beams, without bringing me dreams
   Of the beautiful Annabel Lee;
   And the stars never rise, but I feel the bright eyes
   Of the beautiful Annabel Lee;
   And all through the night, I lie down by the side
   Of my darling, my life and my bride,
   In her sepulcher there by the sea,
   In her tomb by the sounding sea.

One of the favorite themes in blues is that of 'traveling on,' moving from one place to another, finding new loves and new experiences. This restlessness is rarely expressed so well in modern urban blues as in this song by Anne Bredon of San Francisco.

Babe I'm Gonna Leave You

KEY: Bb MINOR   CAPO: 1ST   PLAY: A MINOR

(Dm*) for guitar: May be played by holding Am fingering and sliding up to the 7th and 8th frets, while continuing to play on middle strings.
*As performed: G(F).

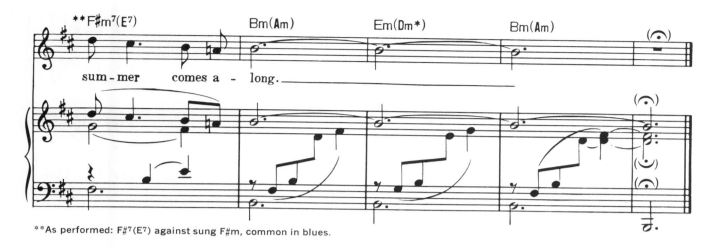

sum - mer   comes a - long. _____

**As performed: F#7(E7) against sung F#m, common in blues.

2.   Babe, that highway's a-callin',
       That old highway's a-callin',
       Callin' me to travel on, travel on out Westward,
       Callin' me to travel on alone.

3.   Babe, I'd like to stay here,
       You know I'd really like to stay here,
       My feet start goin' down, goin' down that highway,
       My feet start goin' down, goin' down alone.

4.   Babe, I got to ramble,
       You know I got to ramble,
       My feet start goin' down and I got to follow,
       They just start goin' down, and I got to go.

Man's yearning for peace is perhaps nowhere better expressed in song than in Ed McCurdy's masterpiece, "Strangest Dream," written in 1950 and now the unofficial anthem of non-political peace groups throughout the English-speaking world.

Last Night I Had the Strangest Dream

KEY: C   CAPO: NONE   PLAY: C

Simply, with dignity

Last night I had the strang - est dream I ev - er had be - fore, I dreamed the world had all a - greed, to put an end to war.

*As performed: G⁷.

**As performed: F.

2. And when the paper was all signed,
And a million copies made,
They all joined hands and circled 'round,
And grateful prayers were made.

And the people on the streets below
Were dancing 'round and 'round,
With swords and guns and uniforms
All scattered on the ground.

3. Last night I had the strangest dream,
I ever had before,
I dreamed the world had all agreed
To put an end to war.

Plaisir d'Amour

This song is the best known composition of Martini il Tedesco, a German-born operatic composer who made his name and fame in his adopted country, France, during the 18th and 19th centuries. The version given here eliminates the developmental sections of the original song, thereby transforming it from a 'through-composed' art song into a strophic folk-like song. The authorship of this English translation is unknown.

KEY: F   CAPO: 1ST   PLAY: E

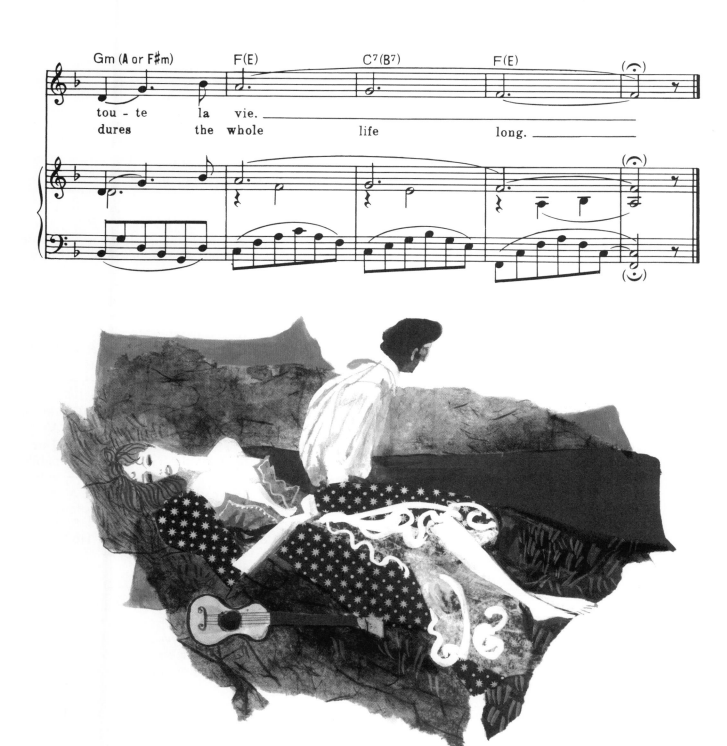

tou - te   la   vie. _____
dures   the   whole   life   long. _____

3. Your eyes kissed mine, I saw the love in them shine,
    You brought me heaven right then when your eyes kissed mine.

4. My love loves me, and all the wonders I see,
    A rainbow shines in my window, my love loves me.

5. And now he's gone, like a dream that fades into dawn,
    But the words stay locked in my heartstrings, "My love loves me."

6. Plaisir d'amour, etc.

The Joan Baez Recordings

JOAN BAEZ
VANGUARD
VSD-2077

Silver Dagger / East Virginia / Fare Thee Well / House of the Rising Sun / All My Trials / Wildwood Flower / Donna Donna / John Riley / Rake and Rambling Boy / Little Moses / Mary Hamilton / Henry Martin / El Preso Numero Nueve.

JOAN BAEZ, VOL. 2
VANGUARD
VSD-2097

Wagoner's Lad / The Trees They Do Grow High / The Lily of the West / Silkie / Engine 143 / Once I Knew a Pretty Girl / Lonesome Road / Banks of the Ohio / Pal of Mine / Barbara Allen / The Cherry Tree Carol / Old Blue / Railroad Boy / Plaisir d'Amour.

JOAN BAEZ IN CONCERT
VANGUARD
VSD-2122

Babe, I'm Gonna Leave You / Geordie / Copper Kettle / Kumbaya / What Have They Done to the Rain / Black is the Color of My True Love's Hair / Danger Waters / Gospel Ship / House Carpenter / Pretty Boy Floyd / Lady Mary / Até Amanhã / Matty Groves.

JOAN BAEZ IN CONCERT, PART 2
VANGUARD
VSD-2123

Once I Had a Sweetheart / Jackaroe / Don't Think Twice, It's All Right / We Shall Overcome / Portland Town / Queen of Hearts / Manhã de Carnaval / Te Ador / Long Black Veil / Fenario / 'Nu Bello Cardillo / With God On Our Side / Three Fishers / Hush Little Baby / Battle Hymn of the Republic

JOAN BAEZ / 5
VANGUARD
VSD-79160

There but for Fortune / Stewball / No, No, No, It Ain't Me, Babe / The Death of Queen Jane / Bachianas Brasileiras No. 5 (Villa-Lobos) / Go 'Way From My Window / I Still Miss Someone / When You Hear Them Cuckoos Hollerin' / Birmingham Sunday / We'll Go No More A-Roving / O Congaceiro / The Unquiet Grave.

BAPTISM—A JOURNEY THROUGH OUR TIME
VANGUARD
VSD-79275

Texts, spoken and sung, by Henry Treece / Walt Whitman / Jacques Prévert (transl. Ferlinghetti) / Federico Garcia Lorca (transl. Spender & Gili) / James Joyce / William Blake / Norman Rosten / John Donne / Anon. / Arthur Rimbaud / Yevgeny Yevtushenko (transl. Milner-Gulland & Levi) / E. E. Cummings / Wilfred Owen / Countee Cullen / From the Chinese (transl. Waley) / From the Japanese (transl. Rexroth).

FAREWELL ANGELINA
VANGUARD
VSD-79200

Farewell, Angelina / Daddy, You Been On My Mind / It's All Over Now, Baby Blue / Will You Go, Laddie, Go / Ranger's Command / Colours / Satisfied Mind / The River in the Pines / Pauvre Ruteboeuf / Sagt mir wo die Blumen sind / A Hard Rain's A-Gonna Fall

NOËL
VANGUARD
VSD-79230

O Come, O Come, Emmanuel / Coventry Carol / The Little Drummer Boy / Down in Yon Forest / The Carol of the Birds / Ave Maria (Schubert) / Mary's Wandering / Away in a Manger / Cantique de Noël / What Child Is This / Silent Night / Instrumentals — Good King Wenceslas / Bring a Torch, Jeannette, Isabella / Angels We Have Heard On High / Deck the Halls / Adeste Fidelis.

JOAN
VANGUARD
VSD-79240

Be Not Too Hard / Eleanor Rigby / Turquoise / La Colombe / Dangling Conversation / The Lady Came From Baltimore / North / Children of Darkness / The Greenwood Sidie / If I Were a Carpenter / Annabel Lee / Saigon Bride.

ANY DAY NOW **(Songs by Bob Dylan)** VANGUARD VSD-79306/7	Love Minus Zero-No Limit / North Country Blues / You Ain't Goin' Nowhere / Drifter's Escape / I Pity the Poor Immigrant / Tears of Rage / Sad-Eyed Lady of the Lowlands / Love is Just a Four-Letter Word / I Dreamed I Saw St. Augustine / The Walls of Redwing / Dear Landlord / One Too Many Mornings / I Shall Be Released / Boots of Spanish Leather / Walkin' Down the Line / Restless Farewell.
DAVID'S ALBUM VANGUARD VSD-79308	If I Knew / Rock Salt and Nails / Glad Bluebird of Happiness / Green, Green Grass of Home / Will the Circle be Unbroken / The Tramp on the Street / Poor Wayfaring Stranger / Just a Closer Walk with Thee / Hickory Wind / My Home's Across the Blue Ridge Mountains.
JOAN BAEZ / **ONE DAY AT A TIME** VANGUARD VSD-79310	Sweet Sir Galahad / No Expectations / Long Black Veil / Ghetto / Carry It On / Take Me Back to the Sweet Sunny South / Seven Bridges Road / Jolie Blonde / Joe Hill / David's Song / One Day at a Time.
CARRY IT ON **Songs from the Original** **Sound-Track of the film** VANGUARD VSD-79313	Oh, Happy Day / Carry it On / "In Forty Days" / Hickory Wind / That was the Last Thing on my Mind / "Life is Sacred" / Joe Hill / I Shall be Released / Do Right Woman, Do Right Man / Love is Just a Four-Letter Word / "Idols and Heroes" / We Shall Overcome
THE JOAN BAEZ **BALLAD BOOK** VANGUARD VSD-41/42	East Virginia / Henry Martin / All My Trials / Old Blue / House of the Rising Sun / Wagoner's Lad / Black is the Color of My True Love's Hair / Lily of the West / Silkie / House Carpenter / The Trees they Do Grow High / Fare Thee Well (10,000 Miles) / Barbara Allen / Jackaroe / John Riley / Matty Groves / Queen of Hearts / Fennario / Go Way From My Window / Railroad Boy / Mary Hamilton / Once I Had a Sweetheart / Silver Dagger
THE FIRST TEN YEARS — **Highlights of the Baez Career** VANGUARD VSD-6560/1	2 Discs including 12 page photohistory With God On Our Side / Don't Think Twice / Goerdie / Te Ador / Green, Green Grass of Home / No Expectations / Sweet Sir Galahad / Turquoise / Farewell Angelina / London (Old Welsh Song) / A Hard Rain's A-Gonna Fall / Ghetto / If I Were a Carpenter / Silver Dagger / Love is Just a Four-Letter Word / There But For Fortune / Will the Circle be Unbroken / John Riley / You Ain't Goin' Nowhere / Mary Hamilton / Carry It On / Manha de Carnaval / If I Knew
BLESSED ARE... VANGUARD VSD-6570/1—STEREO VSQ-40001/2 QUADRAPHONIC	Blessed Are ... / The Night they Drove Old Dixie Down / The Salt of the Earth / Three Horses / The Brand New Tennessee Waltz / Last, Lonely and Wretched / The Slave / Outside the Nashville City Limits / San Francisco Mabel Joy When Time is Stolen / Heaven Help Us All / Angeline / Help Me Make It Through the Night / Let it Be / Put Your Hand in the Hand / Gabriel and Me / Milanese Waltz / Marie Flore / The Hitchhikers' Song / The 33rd of August / Fifteen Months / Deportee (Plane Wreck at Los Gatos) / Maria Dolores

Available on stereophonic discs and in all tape configurations.

Index of Titles

Lyrics to "Outlaw" by Dan Fogelberg

Among the possessions of an outlaw of a low class kind
Is this little bottle of French perfume
Taken as a last thought from a drug store in suburbia
He said, "Lady, look what I've got for you."
She said, "Jesse, I don't hardly even know you anymore.
And judging from your grin, you'd think you held up Henry Ford.
And I don't believe I want you a comin' 'round here anymore. Ooh."

Jesse, he was hurt, boy, and he left there, and he slammed the door.
And he wandered through the alleyways.
Thinkin' all the while that she'd be proud of what he stole for her,
And he tried to think of better ways.
Dreamin' of a movie that he'd seen one afternoon,
He drew out all his savings and he went and bought a gun.
And he ran right home and stood before his mirror
Acting like a thug, ooh.

He waited for a dark night; he was frightened, boy, the fog rolled in,
As a rich man, he came walkin' by,
"Hold your hands up high, " he cried,
"I've come to make your fortune mine."
But his eyes, they gave him right away,
Jesse dropped the gun and they both stared at to where it lay.
And Jesse asked the man if he'd please leave him in his pain.
And the man tried to forgive him, but there's not much he could say. Ooh.

Among the possessions of an outlaw of a low class kind
Is this little bottle of French perfume
Taken as a last thought from a drugstore in suburbia.
He said, "Lady, look what I've got for you."
"Ah, take it, ah, please take it; I'm tired and I'm poor.
And this crappy French perfume is nothin' less than my own soul.
I was feelin' half a man; I wanted to feel whole, ooh

Index
of
Titles

Index of First Lines

Index of First Lines

12/13(188849)